Beautifully Raw™

Inspiring YOU to Eat Raw Food with Raw Chef Wendy

• RAW CHEF WENDY •

HAWAII WAY PUBLISHING

HAWAII WAY PUBLISHING
4118 West Harold Ct., Visalia, CA 93291
www.HAWAIIWAYPUBLISHING.com

HAWAII Way Author/Speakers Agency can send authors to your live event. For more information or to book an event contact HAWAII Way Publishing at: HAWAII WayPublishing@gmail.com, or 559-972-4168.

Printed in the United States of America

ISBN 978-1-945384-03-5

Third edition published in California by HAWAII Way Publishing in July, 2016
Second edition published in Utah by Wendy P. Thueson, Raw Chef Wendy, LLC in 2016
First edition published in Utah by Wendy P. Thueson, Raw Chef Wendy, LLC in 2013
Name changed from 7 Days of Raw Food to Beautifully Raw™: RAWinspiring™ Recipe Series: Author
may be contacted at rawchefwendy@gmail.com

Disclaimer:
The techniques and advice described in this book are a representation of the author's opinions based on her personal experience and are not in any way intended to diagnose, treat, prescribe, or cure any condition you may be experiencing. The author does not in any way claim responsibility for any liability, loss or risk, personal or otherwise, which is incurred as a result of using any of the techniques, recipes or recommendations suggested herein. If in any doubt, or if medical advice is required, please contact the appropriate health practitioner or professional.

To Chad, Hunter, Sadie, Naomi, Cameron and Max

Thank you for your love, patience and support in all that I do.

I love you!

*Photo credits: Heather Walker Photography ™ for portraits and the raw pizza rolls photo.
Wendy P. Thueson for all other food and kitchen photography.*

CONTENTS

WELCOME

Hi, I am Wendy P. Thueson, AKA "Raw Chef Wendy™," and I am so excited to be sharing this recipe book with you. It was originally designed as a One-Week Raw Challenge, but has since evolved into an updated version. This new book, "Beautifully Raw"™ is also used in my new Beautifully Raw™ online program from my RAWinspiring™ recipe series. I have kept the original outline of the book but added more bonus recipes at the end. Many of these recipes also have corresponding videos in the program and upgraded photos.

Whether you want to add more raw food to your current meals or want to dive in and see what this is all about, this guide will help you understand step-by-step how to get started and achieve success.

These Beautifully Raw™ recipes will help you continue on with making new habits for yourself and begin incorporating more of a raw food lifestyle. You may choose to use this book as a one-week challenge or you may use these recipes in your everyday meals by adding other dishes that you usually cook, such as meat, to help yourself and your family transition slowly over to this new lifestyle.

I recommend reducing the amount of meat and dairy you consume for better health by just eating a few bites for the taste.

When I first started eating raw for my health, I had a negative mindset: I looked at all of the foods I could no longer eat and I felt deprived. I noticed I craved these foods even more because of the deep emotional tie I had to food. It helped me to change the way I was thinking about food by looking at all of the beautiful plant foods I could add to what I was eating rather than focusing on what I was subtracting. Being more positive changed my relationship with food for the better.

Whatever you decide, I highly encourage you to add more raw foods to your meals and eat a wide variety of plant-based foods that you and your family will love. I would also like to encourage you to keep in touch as you go through your raw food experience and ask for help when you need it. I am here to help support you in your efforts and help you succeed! Visit www.rawchefwendy.com for more information.

May these recipes inspire you to eat healthier, resulting in greater energy and joy in life.

Wendy ~Wendy P. Thueson | Raw Chef Wendy™ ~

WHAT YOU CAN EXPECT

When I first decided to challenge myself to a full week of raw food, I wasn't doing it for kicks. Having dealt with chronic fatigue for 28 years, brain fog, debilitating neck and back pain, stuttering, Grave's disease, and so many more symptoms made me desperate to find something that could help me in my plight.

I scanned all the raw recipe books I could find in the library. My search for recipes was a long one as I looked for dishes similar to what I was used to eating. As a certified Chef, I was trained to make food look and taste delicious, but this raw food was a whole different world. I had no idea what I was doing with all of these new ingredients and different methods of food preparation. Not cooking food was foreign to me. Determined, however, to try anything to get myself out of the pain and suffering I was experiencing physically, I knew I needed a food make-over but I didn't know where to start, so I just decided to dive in.

That week I turned to simple things like salads, a few raw crackers or chips I could find recipes for, and a lot of fruit and vegetable trays, soaked nuts and seeds. I was busy and I did not want to spend too much time in the kitchen. I found that my body was getting used to not feeling stuffed after a meal of meat and breads and all of the things I used to eat. I felt satisfied and not nearly as hungry as I used to feel. Even though I didn't know what I was doing, my body was getting more nutrition than it had before. Just two days after eating this way, I awoke with energy I had never known before and it sustained itself throughout the day, as long as I ate raw foods. After one week, all of my symptoms were gone and I felt I had been given a second chance at life.

After continuing my research, I realized that when we eat the Standard American Diet (S.A.D.) we are not getting the nutrition our bodies are craving so we keep eating more. However, we end up eating the foods that are quick and easy and that don't have any nutrition due to it being cooked out at high heats. We feel stuffed and tired, but we get hungry again because our bodies cannot find the nutrients they need to create energy and life. It becomes a vicious cycle.

When we choose to eat uncooked fruits, vegetables, sprouted nuts and seeds, however, we end up eating less and the cravings go away because our bodies are flooded with nutrients we can use for energy, repair and healing. Over time, my taste buds have changed to a point that I can't stand the way meat or dairy tastes or even smells. I crave plant-based nutrition because I know I will feel amazing afterward and that is ultimately what my body wants.

I eat to live and have energy and fuel for my body. I love that I feel energetic and light after a meal now instead of heavy and tired. It is amazing to feel so good every day instead of miserable, which was the norm for me before. I have been blessed with a new life through my food choices and I am motivated to create an amazing life and help others to do the same.

This book has been created to help you understand how to incorporate more raw foods into your meals and help transform your lifestyle into one that is healthier, happier and better balanced to suit your needs. You may find that you need to make adjustments. Maybe you need to eat more often or you may find that the meals are not "filling you up." This first week is a big adjustment and you may feel a lot hungrier at first than you have in the past.

In the book "The pH Miracle," by Robert O. Young, PhD, he talks about microforms, which are the fungus, mold, bacteria, etc. in our bodies. When we stop eating the junk food and start eating nutritious foods, the microforms starve. This is the time when cravings come because the microforms are crying out for you to feed them. If you are determined not to give in to the cravings for sweets and other junk, they eventually starve to death and are eliminated from your body. Eating fruits when you want sweets is the best thing to do. We were designed to eat a lot of fruit. This sugar is better for us than the processed sugars we are so used to.

During the first week of eating all raw, I felt hungry all of the time. I ate a lot of fruits, vegetables, nuts and seeds and I ate 6 to 8 times a day. I was also cleaning out a lot, so I needed to stay near a bathroom. It is good to drink a lot of pure water during this time to help the body clean out. Getting through this first week can be a challenge for some people, but each person is different, so you may not experience what I did. I just want to share what I went through to help you understand what could happen. Your results will vary.

"Change Your Mind, Transform Your Body, Experience New Life"

~ Wendy

The Kitchen

THE KITCHEN

We all have different kitchens. Some of them are ideal to work in and others are not. Some are large and spacious and others are small and barely have room to store all we want them to. Whatever your circumstance, you can still make this work. Even if you are in a small apartment, there are ways to maximize your space. Trust me, I've done it!

I am laying it all out here so you can really get an understanding of how I began my Raw Food journey and learn from my mistakes, my challenges and my triumphs. I hope this helps you design your special place in your kitchen and create goals to help achieve the success you are searching for. This picture is of my kitchen. After 15 years, I decided to upgrade my cabinets by painting them white. It gave the room a beautiful, fresh new look and now I love going in there every day. I thought it would help you get a visual of what you can do with your kitchen, if desired. Play around with the space you have and create a sanctuary for preparing and eating your food.

Getting Real

Let's just get it all out on the table right now - my family and I are not perfect. We do not eat 100% raw and we have things in our kitchen that I would rather not have, but there are some battles I just don't want to fight.

Battling over food is not a good idea. People get very emotional over their food and if we try to control it, there can be disorders and other emotional side-effects to these behaviors. I suggest that you provide as much healthy food as possible and allow people to make their choices reasonably. An unreasonable choice would be to eat no fruits and vegetables and only animal products, breads and sweets. This, by the way, was a decision my 5-year-old made to rebel against me, and he paid for it by being backed up for two days and in a great deal of pain. Sometimes nature teaches the lessons a mom tries in vain to teach. He learned the hard way but it was a very effective lesson.

I allow my family to make their own choices and I am the best example I can be to them by eating what makes me feel healthy, energetic and happy. They see this in me and often ask if they can have what I am eating.

I taught my children young how to make salads, vegetable plates, green smoothies, and many more raw food dishes for snacks and meals. My hope is that they will take these good habits with them when they are ready to leave home and venture out on their own.

Some of my children aren't interested in learning how to cook very much. I continue to ask once in awhile if they'd like to help me make dinner or a snack. Sometimes they will and other times they won't. I figure they will come back some day and ask for lessons when they realize they ate better when they lived here than out on their own.

Decide how you want to handle meal times for your family. Getting children involved with the meal preparation is a sure way to get them to eat what you prepare together and try new things. Get them excited about the beautiful, colorful fruits and vegetables and teach them how to make basic recipes from this book. Create family bonding over healthy food to make healthier life-long choices.

STOCKING YOUR KITCHEN

When I first decided to eat raw food, I had to create a space that supported my new lifestyle. As I looked through my kitchen, the pantry, cupboard shelves, refrigerator, freezer and even food storage were full of junk foods, animal products and sugary processed snacks. Feeling overwhelmed, I didn't know where to begin. I wanted to just throw everything out, but it was hundreds of dollars' worth of food.

Re-evaluating my situation, I realized that I was the only one in the family who was determined to make this change. My family was not on board yet because they didn't have a compelling reason like I did. The harder I tried to convince them, the more they resisted. So I was on my own for a while and I needed my own cupboard to support my efforts. I also needed a plan.

I decided to work on myself first and not worry about anyone else. This is similar to the instructions given on an airplane when you are told to take the air mask and use it first, then help others. The realization hit me that I could not convince anyone else until the results I was looking for were achieved. This way I wouldn't have to convince them. They could see for themselves and if they wanted what I had, they could ask. That is exactly what happened. My kids and husband started asking for smoothies, salads and desserts I was making. It worked without me even having to try.

So find a cupboard or shelf you can have just for you and get started. Find some nice containers, if you can, and label them. I used clear ones with lids that fit close together to maximize the space. BPA-free is a good choice and glass containers with plastic lids are even better. You can find coupons for these in the newspaper, so watch for them.

Fruits and vegetables are the best if organic and non-GMO. I realize you may not be able to afford these at first, but please try and think more long-term. This is about prevention down the road. Less doctor visits, medications and sicknesses are often the results people receive from eating healthier. I visit the doctor once a year for a check-up and I am symptom and medication free.

You may also want to start a garden. You can grow an herb garden inside your home all year 'round and a seasonal garden in your yard. This will cut the food bill down quite a bit. It is also helpful to invest in a food dehydrator or freeze dryer to help preserve the food and their enzymes, which is better than canning at high heat. The items in these recipes should be raw - unroasted or uncooked and unsalted.

If you have allergies to any of these foods, choose foods like nuts or seeds that you do not have allergies to. There are always ways to substitute. Please do not feel like you have to purchase all of these items at once. You may add them gradually as needed with the recipes you choose.

The following pages are suggestions for what to stock in different areas in your kitchen. If you do not like something on the list or if you can think of other items, please - or + as needed.

THE COUNTER

I have a corner counter that is large where I put large bowls of a variety of fruits and it has my juicer and other tools to help support my raw lifestyle. Our family of 6 goes through the fruit in this corner in about 3 days. We keep it stocked because this is our medicine!

CUPBOARD OR PANTRY

☐ LEGUMES – Garbanzo beans, green split peas, yellow peas

☐ SEEDS – Sunflower seeds, sesame seeds, raw pumpkin seeds, chia seeds, hemp seeds, flax seeds, buckwheat, amaranth, millet, quinoa, gluten-free oat groats and rolled oats

☐ SPICES – Nutmeg, cinnamon, vanilla, cloves, Kirkland's Organic No-Salt Seasoning [Costco – I use this on a lot of things], cumin, parsley, basil, Italian spice blend, peppercorns, Real™ salt, sea salt or Himalayan salt

☐ SUPERFOODS – Cacao powder, cacao nibs, raw cacao butter, lucuma, maca powder, yacon powder, gogi berries, carob powder and other items you want to have on hand

☐ SWEETENERS – Organic coconut palm sugar, Medjool dates, organic raw honey

☐ OTHER – Raisins, dried cranberries, unsweetened coconut flakes, nutritional yeast

☐ FLOURS – Coconut flour, almond flour, my gluten-free flour blend

REFRIGERATOR

- ☐ VEGETABLES – Celery, carrots, bell peppers, leafy green lettuce, spinach, cucumbers, radishes, Spring mix and other vegetables you love

- ☐ NUT BUTTERS – Raw almond, cashew or other nut butters. *(I stay away from the peanut butters because of the aflatoxin mold they contain. Higher quality peanut butters contain much less of this mold than the cheaper brands. Always get Organic.)*

- ☐ SWEETENERS – Maple syrup

- ☐ SPICES – Garlic, onions, ginger root, turmeric

- ☐ LEFTOVERS – labeled and dated. Throw out after 7 days, if not eaten.

FREEZER

I keep these items in the freezer to last longer and keep them from going rancid. They are also raw – unroasted and unsalted.

- ☐ NUTS – Pecans, walnuts, cashews, macadamias, pine nuts, hazelnuts, almonds

- ☐ FROZEN FRUIT – Berries, fruit mix, peaches, etc.

ORGANIZATION

KITCHEN TRIANGLES

When I designed my kitchen, I read a book my mom gave me called, "Make Your House Do the Housework" by Don Aslett and Laura Aslett Simons that talked about the triangles of the kitchen. This is the most used pathway around your kitchen. For me the main triangle is the refrigerator, the island and the sink. The other areas like the stove and pantry are also a part of it, but this helps me to know where to put my zones.

ZONES

Creating zones in your kitchen will help you move around easier and know how to organize your cupboards and drawers to be more efficient. I have three main zones which create the first triangle called the **Food Prep Zone**. These are the areas of the kitchen that I move around in the most and consist of the **sink,** the **refrigerator,** and the **island**.

The next zone is the **Cooking Zone** which is comprised of the **stove**, the **refrigerator** and the **cupboards** above and below where I put spices, pots and pans, pasta and other cooking ingredients.

Wendy's Kitchen Zones & Triangles

FOOD PREP ZONE

Wendy's Kitchen Zones & Triangles

COOKING ZONE

Wendy's Kitchen Zones & Triangles

BAKING ZONE

Wendy's Kitchen Zones & Triangles

CLEANING ZONE

ZONES

The **Baking Zone** is next with the **pantry** shelves holding my flours, sugars and other baking ingredients, the small **counter-space** next to it - just above the dishwasher, and the **cupboard above** that area as well, which holds the baking spices and raw food ingredients. The island is also a part of this zone because I have cupboards and drawers below the island with baking equipment such as cookie sheets, measuring cups and spoons, spatulas, etc.

The final area is the **Cleaning Zone** which consists of the **sink**, a **cupboard** above for dishes, and the **dishwasher**. This zone is nice because I can do the dishes standing right there and reaching all of what I need to accomplish the task quickly.

If you think about what your needs are and what tools and appliances around the kitchen are needed for each task, you can create your zones accordingly and minimize the amount of time you have to go back and forth from one zone to another. This helps you prepare your food quicker and not be in other peoples' way when they come in and out of the kitchen. It also helps to organize your space and keep the clutter to a minimum. To learn more about zones and see my kitchen in a video, sign-up for my online program by visiting www.rawchefwendy.com where you can view the video in the bonus section.

IDEAS TO INSPIRE

The following areas of my kitchen are ideas for you to possibly implement in your own kitchen if you desire or to get the creative juices flowing and inspire you to do your own thing. Whatever you choose, I suggest you create a space that helps you feel good about being in the kitchen and one that supports this new way of eating.

PANTRY

☐ I have changed over to healthier options for snacks. Cereal is one of those areas I have not demanded to be cut out completely because it is a fight I cannot win right now (even after 7+ years ~ I have rebellious teens in the house). My kids and husband rarely get the sugary kind and I try to find non-GMO cereals, but it can be a challenge. I have an organizer on the door for all of my odds and ends and I like to keep it clean and organized.

☐ I keep my small appliances like my Cuisinart food processor, rice cooker, Kitchen Aid stand mixer, crockpot, air popcorn maker and grain grinder along with my 5-gallon bucket of raw honey at the bottom of the pantry.

☐ On the second shelf I have the kids' dishes and glasses for easy access and some larger plastic containers for storage.

☐ On the third shelf I have the cereals and crackers, etc.

OTHER AREAS OF THE KITCHEN

☐ I have this cupboard next to the pantry on the left side of the sink, above the dishwasher. This is my designated zone in the kitchen for dishes to dry on the counter and for storing the following ingredients: baking spices, sugar substitutes, Blackstrap Plantain Molasses, and other items that I use for making raw desserts and gluten-free desserts on occasion. I also have gluten-free pasta and flours and some packaged gluten-free items.

☐ On the right side of my sink in the corner cupboard above the counter, I have my containers that are labeled with the seeds, Superfoods like maca, lucuma, gogi berries, etc. Dulse [seaweed], and other items I need for preparing my raw dishes. I also have larger bowls to mix with, my mandolin slicer and a few other small tools.

☐ In the cupboard below the same counter in the corner, I have my graduating glass bowls, cheese grater, nut & seed grinder [coffee grinder], and other small tools needed.

☐ In the thin cupboard on the left of the stove, I have my legumes and sprouting supplies, beans, seeds, etc. I also have my salt and pepper grinders, my protein shake, sprouted greens, other supplements and some Dr. Christopher herbal formulas for my children.

☐ To the right of the stove I have all of my spices and paper plates, plastic utensils, etc.

☐ In the island, I have my silverware drawer, knife drawer and other tool drawers. This is where I do most of my raw food preparation, bringing the items from the other cupboards, pantry and refrigerator together.

☐ I keep fruit roll-ups, homemade Green Smoothie roll-ups, dried fruit, raw nuts, granola bars, raisins and other snacks in the cupboard just above my fruit bowl that is always full in the corner.

FOOD PREPARATION TIPS

☐ When I prepare fruits and vegetables I like to have a large bowl available on the counter to put the peels and ends into which will go into my composter outside.

☐ The trash can and recycling should be handy for wrappers and other trash, although eating raw food really cuts down on the trash quite a bit.

☐ Having your knives and cutting boards handy and a wet towel or non-slip mat to go under it is always helpful so the board does not shift when you are cutting.

☐ I do not peel my fruit or vegetables, but on occasion I use a peeler to make my carved fruits and vegetables look good. I use a zester and other tools that are nice to have in one spot as well. These items and measuring cups, spoons, spatulas, knives, etc. are all in my island and are easily accessible when I need them.

☐ To clean off conventional fruit, you can use various products found in the grocery store, which often cause around $2.00+ for a small spray bottle full, or you can make your own [see recipe below].

NATURAL FRUIT & VEGETABLE WASH RECIPE

Yield: ~1 cup or small spray bottle
Ingredients:
1 Tablespoon fresh squeezed organic lemon juice or 3-5 drops lemon essential oil*
2 Tablespoons vinegar
1 cup distilled or pure water

Instructions:
Put all of these ingredients in a BPA-free spray bottle and shake before using. This can be sprayed on the fruit or vegetables and rubbed in a bit, then rinsed off (a much cheaper alternative to those bought in the store).

*I use Purify 100% organic essential oils. See Resources section for more information.

YOU CAN SUCCEED WITH A RAW FOOD LIFESTYLE

1. **CATCH THE VISION OF YOU!** – You don't have to wait to see the results of eating raw food. You can catch the vision and dream big now! Get clear on what you want from raw food and how you will make it happen, then get started.

2. **HOW DO YOU WANT TO LOOK, ACT & FEEL?** What kind of life do you dream of? Envision living that life now. Our minds are powerful and can create what we want. Act AS IF you already live that way and are who you want to become.

3. **EAT TODAY WHAT YOU DREAM OF TOMORROW** – Achieving your dreams starts with small steps toward your ultimate goal. Choose one habit that you want to change regarding food and replace it with a good habit that will sustain and support the lifestyle you want. Then work on that during this week. Add to that a new habit next week and so on.

4. **SUPPORT YOURSELF** – Support yourself by living the lifestyle you want now by eating the right foods. Take time out of your busy schedule for you. Speak and think kindly of yourself and your body. Stay connected to your vision of who you want to become, and act like you are already that person. Your body and mind will follow how you think and how you act.

5. **REACH OUT FOR HELP** – If you get stuck emotionally or otherwise, reach out to a good friend, a person who has been living this lifestyle for a while or me – Raw Chef Wendy. I am happy to help you through the rough patches with the many techniques and tools I have learned. I have many resources to help you fine tune your vision. Consider some one-on-one coaching with me to get where you want to go. Finding a mentor who has been where you are and is now where you want to be is a great way to achieve your dreams faster. If you need help emotionally, please contact me. I am happy to direct you to amazing people I have worked with over the years. You don't need to suffer in silence.

6. **GROW AND ENRICH YOUR EXPERIENCE** – As you change and evolve in your heart, mind, and body, keep the energy in motion by creating new experiences outside what you are comfortable with. Find new friends who relate to the new mindset you have, enrich your relationships by trying new things and nourish yourself physically, mentally, emotionally and spiritually to the highest levels possible. You are worth it!

7. **KEEP A POSITIVE ATTITUDE** – You can do this. When you start to make a change, people all around you can sense the shift from what they are used to. It may make them uncomfortable at first. Reassure them you are doing a good thing for you and them in the long-run. When the negative comments or discouragement come, be ready and have ways to help them become comfortable with the new you. Do not let them get you down because *they* feel a little insecure. This is a good change and you can do it! Be around loving, supportive people and be willing to stand up and ask for what you need and want. You are changing your lifestyle so these shifts will take a little time to get used to but it is also very empowering.

WAYS TO STAY INSPIRED

1. Only eat foods you **LOVE,** but be willing to try new things once in a while.
2. Keep your **VISION** of the NEW you in sight and keep on going.
3. Take care of yourself by practicing ultimate **SELF-CARE!**
4. Find a friend or partner to help **SUPPORT** you and help you get through the rough patches.
5. Look for **BEAUTY** all around you every day and celebrate it.
6. Move your body to **EXERCISE**. Express yourself with dancing and movement.
7. Read inspiring **BOOKS** to enhance your experience and keep you up-to-date on the latest information in your chosen topic.
8. Watch **UPLIFTING** movies or television shows and listen to uplifting music or turn it off all together, which is what I do.
9. Keep a **GRATITUDE JOURNAL** and write down what you are grateful for every day.
10. Do things that **FEED** your **MIND, BODY** and **SPIRIT** in positive ways.
11. Keep a **POSITIVE ATTITUDE** and avoid confrontation.
12. Look for the **GOOD** in all people and all situations. Stay positive.
13. **SERVE** others and forget about yourself.
14. **PLAY** in the kitchen and create new recipes that you make with love.
15. Get **EXCITED** about your new food and encourage others to try it.

ACT AS-IF

Create a new mind and reality shift by acting as-if you are already the person you want to be. This helps you to shift your thinking and begin creating changes you want to see in your behaviors, which will affect the way your mind, body and spirit respond.

Envision the new you and act as-if.

SUCCESS WITH RAW FOOD

1. Drink plenty of purified water throughout the day. Start with a couple of glasses in the morning to hydrate your body inside and out and continue drinking up to 8 glasses a day. Also, when you feel hungry, drink water first to see if you were really thirsty. Sometimes we get these feelings mixed up because they are so closely related.

2. I also suggest drinking distilled water during times of cleansing because it is a "hungry" water and it grabs the inorganic mineral deposits from kidneys, liver, gallbladder and other organs and flushes them out. We get these from hard water and inorganic supplementation. ~ Distilled water does NOT touch the organic minerals we get from plants for the nutrition we need.

3. Drink at least two cups of fresh organic vegetable or green juice daily. This is best at least one hour before a meal or as a meal replacement. Chlorophyll is the energy of the sun and very necessary for an energetic life.

4. Add flaxseed meal, chia seeds, raw/sprouted walnuts and other foods rich in omega 3s to get sufficient amounts in your diet. 1-2 Tablespoons a day added to recipes should do the trick.

5. Include plenty of greens in at least two of your meals, especially dark, leafy greens.

6. Strive to incorporate at least 75% of fruits and vegetables on your plate at every meal. Fruits, salads and raw or lightly steamed vegetables that still have a crunch and bright colors will do wonders to how you feel.

7. If you choose to eat a little meat, choose grass-fed, organic and clean meats and other animal products free of hormones, antibiotics and pesticides. Remember you don't need as much protein as you may think: 5% is all that is needed and this comes from fruits, vegetables, sprouted nuts and seeds. You can thrive on a plant-based lifestyle.

8. Keep your meals simple. At first you may want to mimic the way you are used to eating with fancy raw food dishes that take a lot of time and expensive ingredients to make. You can get just as much nutrition and satisfaction out of simple, delicious meals that don't take a lot of time and frustrate you in the end.

9. If you have a sweet-tooth, keep some raw sweets on hand for those times of weakness. Experiment with new recipes once in a while to keep things new and up-to-date. This should be a fun, new experience for you. Fruit, however, should be the main source of sweets, which is what your body is craving.

10. Soak raw nuts to get rid of the enzyme inhibitors, also call phytic acid. This acid makes it difficult for us to digest raw nuts and some seeds. Soaking for 20 minutes up to 8 hours will help get rid of the bitter taste and actually make the nut taste sweet and the texture soft. All nuts should be soaked and rinsed before using.

INSTRUCTIONS

On the following pages, you will find a Menu Plan, a Shopping List, Recipes and Tracking Sheets for one full week of eating the Raw Food way.

SUBSTITUTIONS: If you happen to come up against any of the following challenges:

- ❖ Food allergies to one or more of the ingredients
- ❖ Not liking an ingredient or two
- ❖ Not being able to find or purchase one or more of the ingredients
- ❖ Not liking the sound of a recipe in the menu

Don't worry. In most recipes, one or more of the ingredients can be substituted with a different ingredient that is similar. For example, if you don't like spinach, use kale, Spring lettuce mix, or any other dark, leafy green lettuce you can find. If you do not like zucchini or cannot find it in a particular time of year, use a different kind of squash for the vegetable noodles or even carrots, beets, or other vegetables you like. Most recipes are easily adapted and may even taste better with your favorite ingredients. There is no right or wrong here. Experiment and have fun in the kitchen and create your own original raw food dishes.

ALTERNATIVES: If a particular recipe does not appeal to you, then find a different recipe that does and go with that. There is no need to feel stuck by having to use ONLY the recipes provided here. There are other wonderful recipes on my website at www.rawchefwendy.com that may look more appealing to you. Choose one or more and go for it! Create your own menu plan, shopping list and recipes if you wish, because you call the shots!

Your body is in a fasting and cleansing state during the night. It is very helpful to continue this cleansing process in the morning when you wake up. I always start my morning with 1-2 green apples and at least one glass of distilled water. Distilled water helps the body clean out the inorganic minerals that have accumulated in various organs and part of the body. The Green Smoothie helps this cleansing process. During the warmer months I often drink a blender full throughout the morning. This gives me plenty of nutrition and added hydration. After my daily workout of alternating running and yoga or lifting weights every other day, I have a protein shake within 30 minutes of my workout to help build the muscles. If you are just starting out, schedule at least a 30 minute walk every day and finish with a plant-based protein shake or snack that does not contain sugar, soy, wheat, dairy or whey, and a large glass of pure water. Then continue with the remainder of the menu and add nourishing snacks as needed. I hope this helps.

~ Raw Chef Wendy

Raw Food Plan

GETTING STARTED

Decide what week you want to begin and mark it on the **calendar**. You may want to be sure to keep your calendar as clear as possible during this first week as you may need to be near a bathroom while your body is naturally cleaning out. 1-2 days before you start you will want to go shopping for your ingredients.

The day before:

- ☐ Gather all of your equipment: A basic blender will do for this menu although a BlendTec® or Vitamix® high-speed blender would be ideal. Be sure you have a cutting board, sharp knife, a spiralizer if possible, and any other equipment stated in the recipes.
- ☐ You may want to make most of these meals ahead of time to free up the rest of the week. They can be made the Saturday or Sunday before for the entire week – except for the smoothies, salad and other items that need to be freshly made.
- ☐ Be sure to label the things you pre-make and date them as you cover and store them in the refrigerator.

The day of:

- ☐ Complete questions on page 25, "Check-in for Day 1" as soon as you wake up. This will only take a few minutes and is very important to record how you are feeling.
- ☐ Follow each recipe as outlined and continue throughout the day.

At the end of the week:

- ☐ Complete questions on page 86, "Check-in for Day 7" as soon as you wake up. If you want to continue eating this way, print out another copy of this page so you can continue recording how you are feeling the next week. You may change up the recipes each week and add others from the Additional Recipes section on pages 92-122.
- ☐ Compare how you feel now to how you felt upon waking the first day using the "Compare & Share" questionnaire. Is there any difference you notice? What specifically did you experience? Record your observations.

CHECK-IN FOR DAY 1:

Please complete this FIRST THING in the morning upon waking before you get started.

On a scale of 1-10, with 10 being the best you can feel, how do you feel upon waking this morning?

(Circle one) 1 2 3 4 5 6 7 8 9 10

Look in the mirror. How does your face look?
1. Blotchy and red
2. Puffy
3. Eyes swollen with dark rings around them
4. Other _____

Stick out your tongue. How pink is it?
1. It is not pink. It is white!
2. Quite pink with some white
3. A nice clean pink with no white
4. Other _____

What kind of mood are you in?
1. Grumpy. I want to go back to bed.
2. Tired. I want to go back to bed.
3. Okay.
4. Happy. I felt like I had a good night's sleep.
5. Energetic! I'm ready to take on the day!
6. Other _____

Please write down any other comments about things you notice upon waking this morning:

_____
_____
_____
_____
_____
_____
_____
_____
_____
_____
_____
_____
_____

LIST OF RECIPES

There are over 100 recipes here to get you eating raw. Eating this way will usually require you to eat more frequently, but you will eat less over time. Remember, you may feel a bit hungrier than usual, but keep going. Eventually you will feel satisfied and be able to go longer periods of time without eating. I hope you enjoy these recipes as much as my family and I do.

SHOPPING LIST FOR THE FULL WEEK

Purchasing organic, wherever possible, is preferable for health reasons and also because they taste much better. If money is an issue, do not let that put you off. You will still find it beneficial to eat this way with conventional fruits and vegetables. As a rule of thumb, buy organic produce that does not have a rind or peel. Lettuce, berries, peppers, etc. are sprayed heavily so these are best organic. Remember too that you will be eating much less than you are used to eating, so the cost of groceries will most likely go down or be about the same as you are used to without all of the meat, dairy and processed foods.

*Please feel free to add any other salads, vegetables, fruits, or sprouted nuts and seeds that you desire for a full meal. You do NOT need to worry about counting calories and watching what you eat if you are eating all raw. Remember, any of the nuts can be substituted for other nuts that you are not allergic to. Play around with the recipes and see what YOU come up with.

FRUIT
- 4 oranges
- 10 lemons
- 2 limes
- 4 Thai coconuts
- 3 cups frozen fruit mix with no sugar added
- 8 bananas
- 1 mango
- 3 cups fresh or frozen raspberries
- 1 cup mixed berries (fresh or frozen with no added sugar)
- 2 cups fresh or frozen pineapple
- 8 Granny Smith apples
- 1 ½ cups each blueberries, peaches or other fruit in season
- 4 cups watermelon
- Variety of fruit like kiwi, strawberries, grapes, apples, bananas, oranges, melons, peaches for fruit kabob

DRIED FRUIT
- 2 ½ cups dried cranberries
- 35-40 Medjool dates
- 3 ½ cups raisins
- ½ cup dried apricots

VEGETABLES

- ☐ 11 cloves garlic
- ☐ ¾ teaspoon fresh ginger
- ☐ ½ cup + 2 Tablespoons yellow or white onion
- ☐ 1 pound leafy greens (you choose: kale, Spring mix, Swiss chard, spinach, etc.)
- ☐ 4 cups fresh salsa, homemade or bought
- ☐ 3 cups fresh guacamole, homemade or bought
- ☐ Olives (black, Kalamata or your favorite)
- ☐ 1 large bunch celery
- ☐ 4 ½ cups carrots
- ☐ 7 cucumbers
- ☐ 1 ½ cups sun-dried tomatoes
- ☐ 4 ¾ cups red or yellow peppers
- ☐ 5 ¾ cups tomatoes (11 or 12 medium tomatoes)
- ☐ 5 cups broccoli florets
- ☐ 1 head cabbage
- ☐ 1 large jicama or turnip to make 1 ½ cups shredded
- ☐ 3 cups fresh spinach leaves
- ☐ 1 head green leaf lettuce
- ☐ 1 handful kale
- ☐ 9 avocados
- ☐ 4 cups red onion
- ☐ 4 ½ cups cilantro
- ☐ 3 cups watercress or parsley or sunflower sprouts (you choose)
- ☐ 2 heads Boston lettuce
- ☐ 1 ½ cups fresh basil
- ☐ ¾ cup fresh parsley
- ☐ 2 ½ cups fresh mint leaves
- ☐ 3 green onions + 3 onion sprigs
- ☐ 2 zucchinis
- ☐ 3 cups red or yellow bell peppers
- ☐ ¼ cup green bell peppers
- ☐ 2 portobello mushroom caps
- ☐ 1 ½ cups parsnips
- ☐ Artichoke hearts
- ☐ Baby portobello mushrooms (optional for pizza)
- ☐ Thai hot pepper or other small chili pepper (optional)
- ☐ 4 cups frozen corn (can't be fresh)
- ☐ 5 yellow squash

NUTS & SEEDS

- ☐ 1 cup + 1 Tablespoon macadamia nuts (or substitute cashews)
- ☐ 1 ½ cup pine nuts (you may substitute cashews if you want)
- ☐ 1 ½ cups almonds
- ☐ 4 cups walnuts (if allergic to walnuts, substitute with a different nut of your choice)
- ☐ 2 ½ cups pecans
- ☐ 10 Brazil nuts or other nut of your choice
- ☐ 3 ½ cups nuts (use walnuts, almonds or pecans, or a combination of these)
- ☐ 4 ¾ cups cashews
- ☐ 3 cups raw or natural peanut or almond butter (or make your own)
- ☐ 1 ½ cups sesame seeds
- ☐ 1 cup raw pumpkin seeds
- ☐ 4 cups flax seeds, whole
- ☐ 3 ¼ cups sunflower seeds
- ☐ ¼ cup black sesame seeds
- ☐ ¾ cup chia seeds
- ☐ 1 ½ cups hemp seeds

GRAINS

- ☐ 11 cups gluten-free rolled oats
- ☐ 2 cups oat flour
- ☐ 1 cup buckwheat
- ☐ 1 cup sprouted quinoa

OILS

- ☐ 1 teaspoon flax oil
- ☐ 3 ¾ cups raw coconut oil
- ☐ 2 ¼ cups + 2 ½ Tablespoons extra virgin olive oil
- ☐ 6 Tablespoons hemp oil or olive oil
- ☐ 2 Tablespoons sesame oil
- ☐ 1/8 cup macadamia oil or coconut oil

SPICES & EXTRACTS

- ☐ 5 Tablespoons cinnamon
- ☐ ¼ teaspoon nutmeg
- ☐ 5 ½ Tablespoons vanilla
- ☐ Sea salt
- ☐ Ground pepper
- ☐ 3 ½ teaspoons Italian seasoning
- ☐ 5¼ teaspoons Kirkland's® Organic No-Salt Seasoning (can get this at Costco)
- ☐ 4 Tablespoons dry mustard
- ☐ ¼ teaspoon turmeric
- ☐ ½ teaspoon mustard powder
- ☐ 3 Tablespoons + 1 teaspoon cumin powder
- ☐ ½ teaspoon cayenne powder
- ☐ ½ teaspoon ginger powder
- ☐ 2 Tablespoons + 1 teaspoon chili powder
- ☐ Pinch paprika
- ☐ 1 tamarind

SWEETENERS

- ☐ 4 ¼ cups raw honey
- ☐ 1 ½ Tablespoons molasses
- ☐ 2 cups maple syrup

MISCELLANEOUS

- ☐ 8 ½ cups coconut flakes, unsweetened
- ☐ ½ cup cacao nibs
- ☐ 2 ½ cups + 1 Tablespoon raw cacao powder
- ☐ 1 ¼ cup Bragg's Liquid Aminos® or coconut aminos
- ☐ ½ cup Bragg's® raw apple cider vinegar
- ☐ 2-3 nori sheets (seaweed)
- ☐ 1 package dulse (seaweed)
- ☐ 1 package round rice paper skins (can find at Good Earth, Whole Foods or Asian market)
- ☐ ¼ cup + 1 teaspoon nutritional yeast
- ☐ 2 Tablespoons miso

INGREDIENTS THAT AREN'T RAW

- ☐ 1 cup organic puffed rice cereal

OPTIONAL SUPPLEMENTATION:

- ☐ 4 scoops Purium® L.O.V.E Shake® mix or Power Shake®
- ☐ Peppermint essential oil (optional)
- ☐ Lemon essential oil (optional)

EQUIPMENT I RECOMMEND

I have purchased equipment over the years or had my husband purchase it for birthdays, Mother's Day, Christmas and other holidays so I can build up my kitchen to support my raw lifestyle. I have listed the equipment I recommend, in order from the most needed to the least. These are very helpful to have. Look for refurbished models. You can get some good deals and they are like new. You can find photos of these at: http://astore.amazon.com/rawchefwendy-20

1. **Cutting board** – I prefer bamboo.

2. **Knife** – a good, sharp Chef's knife (I like the Henckel® knives) that fits well in your hand. You will be using it a lot.)

3. **High speed blender** – I recommend the BlendTec®. I had a Vitamix® and after 4 years, I sold it and got a BlendTec®. The motor is stronger, it's easier to clean, it fits under the cupboards on your countertop, and there is no plunger. The Ninja® is also a decent, more affordable option. Otherwise use what you have but be advised, the regular blenders will give you chunky Green Smoothies. Yuck!

4. **Spiralizer** – I like the Tri-blade®. This is great for making spaghetti noodles out of vegetables.

5. **Coffee grinder** – I use this to grind seeds and spices. I use it often. Be sure to get a sturdy one.

6. **Nut milk bag or sprouting bag** – for making nut milks.

7. **Food Processor** – I recommend the Cuisinart®. I had my first one for 18 years and the plastic broke down but the motor was still going strong. They are great for doing many things.

8. **Dehydrator** – I began with the round $45 one from WalMart®. I had it for a couple of months and traded it for an Excalibur® 9 tray dehydrator. I use it often and I love the large square sheets I can spread crackers, pizza, bread dough, etc. on. There is no hole in the middle to work around and it's flat. Be sure to buy enough Teflex® sheets for each one. I bought 9 total because I use them often.

9. **Juicer** – I recommend the Green Star®. This is excellent for people who need to juice for chronic illness to get the juice into the cells quickly. It can also make nut butters, ice creams, wheat grass juice, and much more. I use the pulp for other recipes and to add to lasagna, etc.

Recipes

BASIC RECIPES

This Menu Plan is unique because it utilizes a few basic recipes to create many dishes. For example, the Whipped Nut Cream is made to be used for several breakfast, snack and dessert recipes. You can make a larger batch of the whipped cream at the beginning of the week and use it throughout the remainder of the week for a variety of recipes. Each recipe will taste unique and delicious. This method, which I call "recipe repurposing," works well to help cut down on cost and preparation time.

WHIPPED NUT CREAM

Yield: 2 cups
Equipment: High-speed blender
Ingredients:
1/2 cup macadamia nuts, soaked 1 hour
1/2 cup pine nuts, soaked 1 hour (you may use cashews if you desire)
1/2 cup purified water
1/2 cup coconut water from a Thai coconut + ½ cup coconut flesh
2 Tablespoons coconut oil
1 teaspoon pure vanilla
1 Tablespoon organic maple syrup

Instructions:
1. Drain the nuts and put in a high-speed blender.
2. Add the remaining ingredients and blend until smooth.
3. Refrigerate until the consistency of whipped cream – overnight is best.
4. Stir with a spoon to be sure it is the right consistency. Let sit in refrigerator until thickened.

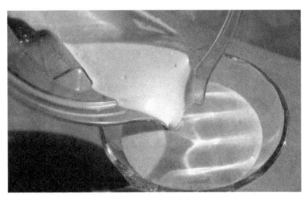

This recipe will be used for the following menu items this week:

Monday – Raspberry Pudding; **Tuesday** – Fruit Bowl with Whipped Nut Cream, Banana Split; **Thursday** – Fruit Platter w/ Creamy Dip, Chia Pudding with Fruit; **Friday** – Breakfast Parfaits; **Sunday** – Green Smoothie Crepes with Whipped Nut Cream & Fruit

---

THAI GINGER SAUCE

Yield: 2 cups
Equipment: Food processor or high-speed blender
Ingredients:
½ cup almonds, soaked overnight
½ cup sesame seeds, soaked 1 hour
¼ cup olive or grape seed oil
¼ cup Bragg's Liquid Aminos® or coconut aminos
¼ cup raw honey or organic maple syrup
1 ½ teaspoons or 2 cloves garlic, minced
¼ teaspoon ginger, grated
1 ¼ cups water (or more for a thinner consistency)
½ teaspoon fresh lemon juice
½ teaspoon curry powder (recipe below)

Instructions:
1. Blend almonds in food processor or high-speed blender until flour-like, if possible. Scrape away from the sides.
2. Add all other ingredients and blend until smooth. It needs to be a sauce consistency for dipping so a little more water may need to be used.
3. Serve with Spring Rolls [recipe on pages 57-58].
4. This recipe is also excellent over noodles or rice, as a sauce in stir-fry, as a dip for vegetables, or as a salad dressing if thinned out a bit more.

> *This recipe will be used for the following menu items this week:*
> **Tuesday** – Thai Veggie Platter; **Wednesday** – Spring Rolls with Thai Ginger Sauce; **Saturday** – Cucumber Rolls with Ginger Sauce

CURRY POWDER*

Yield: ½ cup
Equipment: Coffee grinder, bowl
Ingredients:
½ teaspoon mustard powder
2 Tablespoons cumin powder
1 teaspoon coriander seed powder
¼ teaspoon cayenne powder
½ teaspoon ginger powder

Instructions:
1. Grind all seeds in a coffee grinder until powdered.
2. Mix all ingredients together and put in a spice container with label and date.

*Recipe from Bridget Mars' book, "Rawsome"

BASIC RAW BREAD

Yield: About 24 pieces
Equipment: Coffee grinder (optional), food processor
Ingredients:

1 cup flax seeds, ground
1/3 cup flax seeds, whole
½ teaspoon sea salt
1 clove garlic, minced
2 Tablespoons onion, chopped
1 1/3 cups water
2/3 cup sunflower seeds, soaked 2 hours or more and rinsed
¼ cup black sesame seeds
1 teaspoon Italian seasoning
½ teaspoon Kirkland's® Organic No-Salt Seasoning

Instructions:

1. In a coffee grinder, grind the 1 cup flax seeds to a meal and place in a medium bowl.
2. Add the remaining ingredients and mix together well.
3. This will make chunky consistency bread. For smoother bread you may put in a food processor and process until smooth.
4. Put ½ the mixture on a Teflex® sheet which is on top of the mesh tray and spread to about ¼ of an inch thickness.
5. Dehydrate on 105 F. about 4 hours and turn over onto another Teflex® sheet.
6. Score into squares with a knife, being careful not to cut into the sheet, and dehydrate an additional hour.
7. Then remove from tray and use or put in a bag in the refrigerator.

This recipe will be used for the following menu items this week:
Monday – Veggie Burger; **Thursday** – Crispy Dulse Sandwich; **Friday** – Raw Pizza

GREEN SMOOTHIE

Yield: 4-6 servings
Equipment: High-speed blender
Ingredients:
4 large handfuls of fresh leafy greens (kale, Spring mix, Swiss Chard, spinach, etc. or a combination of these)
1 ½ – 2 cups fresh fruit or frozen fruit blend with no added sugar
1 banana
1 cup ice (optional)
1 teaspoon chia seeds
1 Tablespoon flax seeds
½ – 2 cups water or fresh fruit juice

Instructions:
1. Blend all ingredients in high-speed mixer.
2. Serve.

> *This recipe will be used for the following menu items this week:*
> This can be made anytime throughout the week for a snack or breakfast and will be dehydrated for the Green Smoothie Roll-ups that can also be used as a snack; **Sunday** – Green Smoothie Roll-us for Crepes

GREEN SMOOTHIE ROLL-UPS

Yield: 6-8 roll-ups
Equipment: High-speed blender and dehydrator
Ingredients:
1 recipe Green Smoothie

Instructions:
Take your Green Smoothie mixture from the recipe above and spread about 1/4 of an inch thick on a Teflex® sheet on a tray and out it in the dehydrator overnight, or until completely dry and pliable. Rip from the Teflex® sheet and cut with clean scissors into 4 squares. Roll them up and wrap with plastic for a quick on-the-go snack. My kids and their friends love them and I enjoy them too. Just be sure to brush your teeth afterward so the sugar doesn't sit on them.

> *This recipe will be used for the following menu items this week:*
> **Sunday** – Green Smoothie Crepes with Whipped Nut Cream and Fruit

MONDAY

Breakfast

GRAWNOLA

Yield: 1 gallon
Equipment: Food processor, dehydrator
Ingredients:
4 cups gluten-free oat flakes
1 cup flax seeds
½ cup hemp seeds
1 Tablespoon chia seeds
1 cup sunflower seeds, soaked and drained
½ cup sesame seeds, soaked and drained
1 Tablespoon cinnamon
½ cup walnuts, soaked, drained and chopped
½ cup pecans, soaked, drained and chopped
½ cup coconut, flaked with no sugar
½ cup Medjool dates, pitted and chopped
1 teaspoon flax oil
4 Tablespoons raw honey
2 Tablespoons raw coconut oil
1 ½ Tablespoons molasses
½ cup organic maple syrup
Juice of 3 oranges, about 3/4 cup
1 cup dried cranberries, soaked and drained

~ Instructions on next page ~

Instructions:

1. Prepare all nuts and fruit to be soaked 1 hour ahead of time; or if you are in a rush, soak just before starting the recipe and put in very last. They can also be soaked overnight.
2. In a saucepan on low heat, melt the raw honey and coconut oil until just melted. Do not overheat.
3. Put everything in a bowl and mix well. Pour honey and oil mixture over ingredients and blend with your hands.
4. Spread out between several dehydrator trays and dehydrate overnight, stirring occasionally until completely dry.
5. Enjoy with hemp milk or almond milk as a cereal, eat by the handfuls on the run, or mix with other dried fruit for a trail mix. Refrigerate or freeze for long term storage, if it lasts that long!

ALMOND MILK

Yield: 4 cups
Equipment: High-speed blender
Ingredients:
1 cup raw almonds
4 cups pure water
2-3 Medjool dates, pitted (optional)
½ teaspoon vanilla (optional)

Instructions:

1. Blend almonds and water in a high-speed blender until smooth.
2. Strain mixture through a cheesecloth or a nut milk bag.
3. Do NOT throw away the almond meal. This can be used for the coconut macaroon recipe on **Wednesday**. It is good for any recipe with almond meal or flour in it.

*For a sweeter milk add 2-3 dates before blending and ½ teaspoon vanilla.
*Other nuts may be used; Brazil nuts are high in selenium; chestnuts or other nuts may be substituted as well.

GREEN PROTEIN SHAKE

I found Purium® after a long search for a gluten-free, vegan, dairy-free, egg-free, soy-free, wheat-free and 100% all natural protein shake mix. I wanted this and powdered sprouted greens that would be quick and easy to mix and drink after a workout or in place of breakfast when I was in a hurry. I use this in my shake. It is optional. If you prefer, add a couple handfuls of lettuce greens instead.

Yield: 1 ½ cups
Equipment: High-speed blender
Ingredients:
8 ounces pure water
1 scoop Purium® L.O.V.E.® or Power Shake® powder mix*
1 large banana
1 cup ice

Instructions:

1. Put ingredients into the blender in order given.

2. Blend until smooth.

3. Add water if too thick or if adding more fruit, until desired consistency is achieved.

4. Pour into a glass and drink.

See resource section for information on this product.

Lunch

LARGE MEXICAN SALAD

Yield: 1 serving

Ingredients:

2-3 handfuls green leafy lettuce or other mixed greens

Handful of sprouts (mung bean, alfalfa, etc.)

½ cup fresh guacamole

½ cup fresh salsa

6-8 olives (black, Kalamata, or other)

Instructions:

1. Fill a large dinner plate full of leafy greens. You may choose from Spring Mix, green leaf lettuce, Romaine lettuce, or whatever you have on hand. I stay away from Iceberg lettuce because it doesn't really have much nutritional value.

2. Add the following on top of the lettuce: mung bean sprouts or other sprouts you have on hand, diced avocado or fresh guacamole (I make mine by mashing up 1 avocado and adding fresh salsa and some lime or lemon juice), fresh salsa, olives, and red or green onions, diced.

3. This makes a great meal. You can put corn tortilla chips on top if you desire [recipe on page 75].

Snack

ANTS ON A LOG

Yield: As many as you want

Ingredients:

Celery stalks

Raw almond butter

Raisins

Instructions:

1. Take several celery stalks, wash, cut and spread raw almond butter on top.
2. Add raisins for the ants.
3. This is a great treat for kids too! They love eating this simple treat. It is packed with fiber and protein as well!

Dinner

VEGGIE BURGER

Yield: 4 servings
Equipment: Food processor
Ingredients:

2 stalks celery, chopped
½ small carrot, shredded or chopped
¼ cup onion, diced
1 clove garlic, minced
1/8 cup sun-dried tomatoes
1 Medjool date, pitted
½ cup red or yellow bell pepper, diced
1 teaspoon sea salt
2 teaspoons Italian spice blend
½ teaspoon Kirkland's® Organic No-Salt Seasoning
1 cup sunflower seeds, ground
½ cup flax seeds, ground
1 Tablespoon hemp seeds
Hamburger toppings: sliced red onion, sliced tomatoes, pickles, mushrooms, lettuce
1 recipe Basic Raw Bread on page 38.

Instructions:

1. Blend all ingredients in a bowl in the order they appear. You may choose to hand chop everything and have a chunky looking burger or place each ingredient in a food processor and chop it fine for more of a burger texture.

2. Mix well and form 4 individual balls and flatten them like hamburgers.

3. Serve on top of the Basic Raw Bread [recipe on page 38] and top preferred hamburger toppings, Raw Ketchup and Raw Mustard Sauce [recipes on page 46].

4. These patties can be put in the dehydrator for a couple of hours to firm them up and get some of the moisture out and have more of a 'cooked' texture.

RAW KETCHUP

Yield: 2 cups
Equipment: High-speed blender
Ingredients:
1 tomato, diced
3 Tablespoons date paste (pit about 3 Medjool dates and process in food processor with 1 Tablespoon water until smooth)
½ cup sun-dried tomatoes
¼ cup extra virgin olive oil
1 Tablespoon raw apple cider vinegar
1 teaspoon sea salt
¼ teaspoon Kirkland's®Organic No-Salt Seasoning
6 Tablespoons pure water

Instructions:
1. Blend all ingredients, in order, in a high-speed blender until smooth.
2. Use immediately or refrigerate up to four days.

RAW MUSTARD SAUCE:

Yield: 1 ½ cups
Equipment: High-speed blender
Ingredients:
1 Tablespoon Medjool dates, pitted
2 Tablespoons water
4 Tablespoons dry mustard
1 Tablespoon pure water
2 Tablespoons raw apple cider vinegar
2 Tablespoons fresh squeezed lemon juice
2 drops lemon essential oil (optional)
A pinch of turmeric for color
1 cup extra virgin olive oil

Instructions:
1. Soak the dates in the water for about 20 minutes, then drain off water. Add to the high-speed blender.
2. Add the remaining ingredients except the olive oil, and blend until smooth. Slowly add the olive oil until incorporated.
3. Use immediately or refrigerate up to four days.

Dessert

RASPBERRY PUDDING

Yield: 4-6 servings

Equipment: High-speed blender

Ingredients:

3 cups fresh or frozen raspberries

1 mango, peeled, pitted and diced

1 Medjool date, pitted

2 Tablespoons maple syrup

1-2 cups Whipped Nut Cream [recipe on page 36]

Instructions:

1. Place all of the ingredients, except for the whipped cream, in a high-speed blender and blend until smooth.

2. In a bowl or fancy dessert glass, place some of the whipped cream and then the raspberry sauce on top. Then take a knife and swirl the two together just slightly to create a beautiful swirled effect.

3. Serve immediately or chill first, then serve.

TUESDAY

Breakfast

FRUIT BOWL WITH CREAM

Yield: 1 serving

Ingredients: Fresh mixed fruit, whipped nut cream for topping

Instructions:

Fill a bowl with a variety of fruit and add Whipped Nut Cream on top [recipe on page 36]. Enjoy for breakfast or any time of the day.

BERRY PROTEIN SHAKE

Yield: 1 blender full

Equipment: Blender, a regular one is fine.

Ingredients:

8 ounces pure water

1 scoop Purium® Shake powder mix of your choice (optional)

1 large banana

1 cup mixed berries

1 cup ice

Instructions:

1. Put ingredients into the blender in order given.

2. Blend until smooth

3. Add water if too thick or if adding more fruit, until desired consistency is achieved.

4. Pour into a glass and drink up!

Lunch

NORI ROLLS

Yield: 8-12 rolls
Equipment: Sushi mat
Ingredients:

'Rice':

1 ½ cups jicama or turnips, peeled and diced
½ cup pine nuts or cashews, soaked for 30 minutes
2 teaspoons raw apple cider vinegar
¼ teaspoon sea salt

Filling:

Handful of spinach leaves
½ cup red peppers, julienned
½ cup carrots, julienned
1 avocado, sliced thin
½ cup red onion, cut into thin strips
Handful cilantro
Handful watercress or parsley or sunflower sprouts

Wrappers:

2-3 nori sheets (seaweed)

Instructions:

1. Place 1 nori sheet on a sushi mat or other pliable surface that can be rolled.
2. Spread a small amount of 'rice' on the bottom going almost to the edges of the entire nori roll.
3. Top with a small amount of the filling ingredients, being careful not to add too much, but covering the 'rice' on the bottom layer.
4. Roll up by starting at the long edge closest to you and pushing the mat away from you as you roll. You should be able to see the layers as you roll.
5. Cut into bite-sized pieces and arrange on a plate. Enjoy!

Snack

DATE BOATS
Yield: As many as desire.
Ingredients:
Raw nut butter of your choice or a soaked nut (I use almond butter or soak any kind of nut like pecans, walnuts or almonds for 3-8 hours or overnight and use it in place of the butter)
Medjool dates
Coconut, unsweetened and shredded (optional)

Instructions:
1. Open the dates lengthwise and take out the pit.
2. Put the two halves on a plate and fill with nut butter or a soaked nut.
3. You may also roll it in unsweetened shredded coconut for an added layer of flavor.
4. Serve.

This quick and easy snack will satisfy any sweet-tooth
and give you energy to get through the afternoon.

Dinner

THAI LETTUCE WRAPS

Yield: About 6-8 wraps
Equipment: Saucepan, knife and cutting board
Ingredients:
2 heads Boston lettuce

Fillings:
1 ½ - 2 cups each julienned carrots, julienned red and yellow peppers, julienned red onions, and sunflower sprouts, cilantro, basil and/or mint leaves

Nut Filling:
2 cups cashews, soaked and rinsed
2 Tablespoons Braggs Liquid Aminos® or Coconut Aminos
1 Tablespoon green onions, diced
2 teaspoons curry powder [recipe on page 37]
3 1/4 cups Thai coconut milk and meat

Instructions:
For Platter:
1. Core the washed lettuce and take each large leaf and put it on a large platter. These will act as the edible bowls.
2. Put each of the julienned fillings in each of the edible leaf bowls and arrange, varying the colors for a nice visual appeal.

~ Instructions on next page ~

3. Put the Thai Ginger Sauce [recipe on page 37] in a small bowl in the center of the platter for dipping.
4. Place remaining large lettuce leaves on the sides of the platter for wraps.

For Nut Filling:
1. Take ½ cup of the soft cashews and blend with the coconut milk and meat in a blender until smooth to make a sauce. DO NOT BLEND ALL THE CASHEWS. I created this recipe to be a substitute for chicken, so the nuts give the nice look of diced chicken that I was going for.
2. In a saucepan on low heat, add remaining ingredients and warm, using the finger as a guide.
3. Serve warm in the edible lettuce bowls in the center of the platter.

For Serving:
1. To eat, have platter in the center of the table and have people take one of the lettuce leaves and add some of each of the fillings and roll up the leaf into a wrap.
2. The sauce is for dipping. You may want to have a small bowl of sauce for each person to dip their own wraps.

Dessert

RAW NANAIMO BARS

Yield: 9 servings
Equipment: Food processor
Ingredients:

Layer One:

1 ½ cups nuts (walnuts, almonds, or pecans or a combination of these), soak overnight
1/3 cup coconut, unsweetened and shredded
8 Medjool dates, pitted
1 Tablespoon organic maple syrup
1 Tablespoon raw cacao powder

Layer Two:

1 cup raw nut butter (I use almond)
3 Tablespoons coconut oil
3 Tablespoons organic maple syrup
½ vanilla bean or 1 teaspoon vanilla
2-3 drops peppermint essential oil (optional)

Layer Three:

½ cup coconut oil
¾ cup raw cacao powder
6-7 Medjool dates, pitted
1 avocado, mashed
1 teaspoon pure vanilla
½ cup organic maple syrup

Instructions:

1. Combine each layer separately in the food processor and press one at a time into a 9"x 9" pan.
2. Chill until firm
3. Cut into small squares.

*These layered bars are a little time consuming but they are worth it! Your family will love them.

WEDNESDAY

Breakfast

PINEAPPLE/BANANA SMOOTHIE
Yield: 1 blender full
Equipment: High-speed blender
Ingredients:
2 cups fresh or frozen pineapple
2 handfuls fresh organic spinach
1 banana
1 Tablespoon each chia, hemp & flax seeds
½ – 2 cups purified water (use more for a thinner drink)

Instructions:
Blend in a high-speed blender until smooth. Enjoy!

*Purium® Shake and greens can be added to this for more nutrition.
What a great way to pack your day by starting with a power drink.

$\mathcal{S}nack$

APPLE CRISP

Before starting this recipe, gather the ingredients and soak the nuts & raisins in purified water. Prepare everything in a bowl and rinse the nuts and raisins just before using. That should be plenty of soaking time to get the enzyme inhibitors off the nuts and soften the raisins.

Yield: 9 servings
Equipment: Food processor
Ingredients:
Filling:
7 Granny Smith apples, cored and diced
2 1/2 Tablespoons lemon juice
2 1/2 Tablespoons organic maple syrup
1/2 teaspoon cinnamon

Topping:
1/2 cup raw walnuts or pecans, soaked & drained
1 cup buckwheat, soaked overnight and drained
1/2 cup raisins, soaked & drained
1/4 cup coconut oil
4 teaspoons maple syrup
1 teaspoon cinnamon
Dash nutmeg
1/2 teaspoons sea salt

Instructions:
Filling:
1. Mix together in a bowl.
2. Spread in an 8"x8" baking dish.

Topping:
1. Chop the nuts and raisins in a food processor until small chunks form. Add the rest of the ingredients except the buckwheat.
2. Transfer to the bowl you made the filling in, and mix in buckwheat by hand.
3. Sprinkle over the filling until covered.
4. Place pan in a dehydrator with the shelves taken out. Dehydrate at 105 degrees F. until warm, about 1-2 hours.
5. Serve from the pan warm with a little Whipped Nut Cream on top for dessert, or any other time [recipe on page 36].

Lunch

SPRING ROLLS

Yield: 6-8 servings

Equipment: Mandolin or knife and cutting board

Ingredients:

16 – 8 ½" round rice paper skins from any Asian market

½ pound mixed lettuce greens (spring mix, romaine, green or red leaf lettuce, etc.) or Napa cabbage

2 carrots, peeled and julienned

½ cucumber, peeled and julienned

¼ cup scallions, julienned

1 bunch cilantro, washed

1 bunch basil, washed

2 avocados, sliced in thin strips

1 red pepper, sliced in thin strips

Celtic salt & fresh ground black pepper to taste

Thai Ginger Sauce [recipe on page 37]

~ Instructions on next page ~

Instructions:

1. Wash lettuce and tear into small pieces.
2. When all vegetables are prepared and laid out in front of you, fill a shallow cake pan with warm water.
3. Put three rice paper circles in water. They will become soft, but don't allow to stay in water too long as they will get too soft. Work quickly.
4. Pull out 1 rice paper circle and put it on a cutting board. On the bottom 1/3 section place 4-5 leaves of cilantro and 2-3 leaves basil. On top of these leaves, lay a couple of slices of avocado, red pepper, cucumber and 2-3 carrots.
5. Add a handful of lettuce and roll up the spring roll.
6. Lift the bottom edges up over the pile with one hand, and hold the vegetables in place tightly with the other.
7. Fold the left side over, then the right and tightly roll the rest of the spring roll until everything is enclosed.
8. Continue with all of the rice papers and vegetables.
9. Eat them as soon as possible with the delicious Thai Ginger Sauce or refrigerate until your guests get there.

Snack

CHOCOLATE DOUGHNUT HOLES

Yield: 2 dozen

Equipment: Food processor

Ingredients:

2 cups nuts of your choice (pecans, Brazil nuts or walnuts)

1 cup raw flaked oats

2 cups oat flour made from raw oat groats

1/3 cup coconut oil, softened but not melted

1/3 cup organic maple syrup

1 teaspoon cinnamon

Dash nutmeg

¼ cup shredded coconut (to roll them in)

1/8 cup raw cacao or carob powder

Instructions:

1. In a food processor, grind dry nuts. [These are optimal soaked first for 30 minutes and dried for several hours or overnight, then processed.]
2. Combine dry ingredients, then combine wet ingredients and mix well.
3. Form into balls and roll in shredded coconut.
4. Put on a platter and serve.

Dinner

VEGETABLE SPAGHETTI WITH PESTO SAUCE

Yield: 2 servings
Equipment: Spiralizer® or Saladaco®
Ingredients:
2 zucchini

Pesto:
½ cup fresh basil leaves, packed
¼ cup each parsley leaves and mint leaves, packed
¼ cup pine nuts or pistachios
2 Tablespoons olive oil
½ clove garlic, minced
½ teaspoon sea salt
Pinch black pepper

Topper:
½ teaspoon nutritional yeast

Instructions:

1. Make vegetable noodles with the Spiralizer® by cutting the ends off the zucchini and cutting it in half. Put the zucchini in the spiralizer with the end closest to the blade and turn handle, pushing slightly. Make sure the blades are in the correct position – follow manufacturer's directions.
2. For pesto, put all ingredients in a food processor and blend until slightly chunky.
3. You may warm the noodles in a saucepan with a Tablespoon of olive oil on low heat, add the pesto and mix around until just warm to the touch. It is best doing this right before serving.
4. Garnish with leaves from mint or parsley.
5. Sprinkle with a little nutritional yeast for a cheesy flavor.

Dessert

COCONUT MACAROONS

Yield: About 18 cookies

Equipment: Food processor, dehydrator

Ingredients:

3 cups raw coconut, shredded and unsweetened

3 Medjool dates, pitted

¼ cup raw honey or maple syrup

1 teaspoon vanilla

Instructions:

1. Blend all ingredients in food processor until mixed well.
2. Form balls with scoop or by hand.
3. Dehydrate at 105 F. for 4-6 hours or longer for more crunchiness, or eat them as is.

These little balls of joy melt in your mouth. They look wonderful on a tray for serving and are very tempting to the palate. Make a tray of them and take them to the next social event you have. No one will know they are "RAW."

THURSDAY

Breakfast

CHIA PUDDING WITH FRUIT

Yield: 2 ½ cups

Ingredients:

1 ¾ cups Whipped Nut Cream [recipe on page 36]

½ cup chia seeds

1/8 cup Almond Milk [recipe on page 41] or purified water

¼ to ½ cup organic maple syrup or raw honey (depending on how sweet you like it)

1 teaspoon vanilla

½ teaspoon cinnamon

Dash nutmeg

1 cup each blueberries and peaches or other fruit on hand, diced

Instructions:

1. Mix whipped cream with chia seeds, sweetener of your choice, vanilla and cinnamon. Set aside.

2. Cut peaches into small cubes.

3. When chia pudding is thick, about 10 minutes, stir in fruit or put on top with a little whipped nut cream to garnish and a mint leaf if you have one on hand.

4. Refrigerate leftovers.

Snack

PEACH COBBLER PROTEIN SHAKE

Yield: 4-6 servings
Equipment: High-speed blender
Ingredients:

1 banana
1 scoop Protein Shake Powder (optional)
1 teaspoon cinnamon
1 teaspoon vanilla
1 cup Almond Milk [recipe on page 41]
2 cups peaches
Ice

Instructions:

1. Blend all ingredients in order they appear until smooth.
2. Enjoy!

Lunch

WATERMELON GAZPACHO

Yield: 6 ½ cups
Equipment: Blender or food processor
Ingredients:

3 cups watermelon, seeded and pureed in a blender or food processor
1 cup watermelon, seeded and diced small
1 cup tomato, seeded and diced small (about 2 medium tomatoes)
1 cup cucumber, peeled, seeded and diced small
¼ cup red bell pepper, diced
¼ cup green bell pepper, diced
2 Tablespoons lime juice
1 small handful cilantro leaves, chopped
½ small jalapeno, seeded and minced
1 green onion, white and green minced
1 teaspoon sea salt
Fresh ground pepper

Instructions:

1. In a large bowl, combine the ingredients as listed and stir to combine.
2. Season with pepper and salt to taste.
3. Refrigerate to chill, then serve in individual bowls.
4. Add more hot peppers if you like more heat. Serve in a bowl or as an hors d'oeuvre in a hollowed out cucumber cup.

Snack

FRUIT KABOBS WITH CREAMY DIP

Yield: As many as desire

Equipment: High-speed blender

Ingredients:

Kabobs:

A variety of fruit such as kiwi, strawberries, grapes, apples, bananas, oranges, melons, etc. cut into large chunks and arranged on small skewers and put on a platter.

Creamy Dip:

1 cup of Whipped Nut Cream [recipe on page 36]

¼ cup peaches

¼ cup strawberries

2 Tablespoons raw honey or organic maple syrup

1 teaspoon vanilla

½ teaspoon cinnamon

1 Tablespoon fresh squeezed orange juice

Instructions:

1. Place all ingredients for Creamy Dip in a high-speed blender and blend until smooth.
2. Transfer to a small bowl for dipping kabobs.

Dinner

REUBEN ROLL WITH THOUSAND ISLAND DRESSING

Yield: 12 wraps

Ingredients:

Filling:

2 portobello mushroom caps, stems removed and sliced into julienne strips of about ¼"

½ red onion, thinly sliced

1 Tablespoon olive oil

1 Tablespoon Bragg's Liquid Aminos® or Nama Shoyu

1 Tablespoon fresh squeezed lemon juice

Dash sea salt

Dressing:

1 cup cashews, soaked 30 minutes and drained

½ cup sun-dried tomatoes, chopped

1 red bell pepper, seeded and chopped

1 cup celery, chopped

2 Tablespoons olive oil

1 Tablespoon miso

¼ cup fresh squeezed lemon juice

2 Tablespoons raw apple cider vinegar

1 Tablespoon honey or organic maple syrup

½ clove garlic, minced

1 cup pure or distilled water

Sea salt and ground pepper to taste

Wrap:

6 large Swiss chard leaves with the stems removed and sliced in half

1 cup fresh sauerkraut (Bubbie's® brand is great, or do it yourself)

Instructions:

1. Make a marinade out of the ingredients listed under FILLING except for the mushrooms. Toss mushrooms in the marinade and allow to sit for 30 minutes before serving.

2. Make the dressing out of the ingredients under DRESSING in a high-speed blender and season with salt and pepper to taste.

3. Place a leaf of Swiss chard on a plate and fill with sauerkraut and a few marinated mushroom slices. Drizzle with dressing before wrapping, or use dressing as a side dip.

SAUERKRAUT

Yield: 1 quart
Ingredients:
1 head cabbage
1 Tablespoon sea salt

Instructions:
1. Remove core and shred entire cabbage.
2. Place in a bowl and pour salt over it. Work it in with your hands, kneading and squeezing it until liquid begins coming out.
3. When it has reduced by half, pack the salted cabbage in layers into a 1 quart canning jar, pressing each layer down as much as you can. The entire amount of cabbage should fit into a quart jar.
4. The liquid should be over the sauerkraut. Pour some of the liquid from the bowl if you need room for more cabbage.
5. Loosely cap the jar and put into a dark place in your kitchen. Check it every other day and skim off the top layer (bloom) if needed, pressing the kraut below the liquid if needed. After 2 weeks, check it and see if the taste is to your liking. You may continue fermenting it, or put it in the refrigerator and use.

Dessert

CHOCOLATE PUDDING

Yield: 4-6 servings
Equipment: High-speed blender
Ingredients:
2 avocados, mashed
1 cup coconut milk
¾ cup raw honey or maple syrup
1 cup cacao powder
2 teaspoons vanilla
¼ teaspoon cinnamon
Pinch of sea salt

Instructions:
1. Blend in a high-speed blender until smooth.
2. Chill in the refrigerator to set a bit in a large bowl.
3. Serve in the serving dishes.

FRIDAY

BREAKFAST PARFAITS

Yield: 1 serving

Ingredients:

½ cup raw granola [*Graw*nola recipe on pages 40-41]

½ cup Whipped Nut Cream [recipe on page 36]

½ cup mixed fruit, cut into chunks

Instructions:

1. In a parfait glass, layer a tablespoon or two of the whipped cream at the bottom.
2. Add a tablespoon or two of the fruit and then the granola.
3. Repeat until the glass is full and serve.

MINT CACAO MILKSHAKE

Yield: 2 servings

Equipment: High-speed blender

Ingredients:

½ cup young Thai coconut meat

¼ cup raw honey or organic maple syrup

1 teaspoon vanilla

¼ cup cacao powder

1 cup Almond Milk [recipe on page 41]

1 cup young Thai coconut milk

10 fresh mint leaves

5 drops peppermint essential oils (optional)

Cacao nibs and mint leaves for garnish

Instructions:

1. In a high-speed blender, blend all ingredients, except garnishes, until smooth.
2. Pour into glasses and serve.

Lunch

QUINOA VEGETABLE TABOULEH

Yield: 4 servings
Equipment: Quart jar with mesh lid or cheesecloth for sprouting
Ingredients:

4 cups diced cucumber (remove the seeds if very large)
3 cups cilantro leaves, roughly chopped
¼ cup fresh parsley, chopped
2 Tablespoons fresh mint leaves, chopped
1 ¾ cups heirloom tomatoes, diced
¾ cup red bell peppers, diced
½ cup hemp seeds
¼ cup sweet onion, diced
¼ cup freshly squeezed lemon juice
6 Tablespoons hemp oil
2 cloves of garlic, minced
1 teaspoon sea salt
Fresh ground pepper to taste
1 cup sprouted quinoa [see directions below]

Instructions:

1. 1-2 days ahead, sprout your organic quinoa by rinsing it and placing it in a bowl. Cover quinoa with pure water and let soak 4-6 hours.
2. Drain the water and rinse the quinoa.
3. Put the quinoa back in the bowl or a sprouting jar with mesh lid and let them grow.
4. Continue rinsing the next 1-2 days both morning and night and they will be done when the little tails are growing.
5. Growing them longer than 2 days will make them lose some of their nutrition and they will lose their crunch.
6. Mix remaining ingredients for Tabbouleh together in a bowl and serve.

Snack

GREEN SMOOTHIE ROLL-UPS [recipe on page 39]

Dinner

RAW PIZZA
Yield: 4-6 servings
Equipment: Dehydrator, high-speed blender or food processor
Ingredients:
Crust:
Basic Raw Bread [recipe on page 38], cut into individual squares

Sauce:
2 large tomatoes, diced
¼ cup sun-dried tomatoes
2-3 Tablespoons onion, diced
2 whole Medjool dates, pitted
½ clove garlic, minced
1 teaspoon Kirkland's® Organic No-Salt Seasoning
½ teaspoon Italian seasoning blend

Toppings:
1 cup each of the following: sun-dried tomatoes in strips or diced; red or yellow peppers, diced; red or green onions, diced; black or Kalamata olives, sliced; artichoke hearts, diced; mushrooms, sliced

Instructions:
1. Chop both kinds of tomatoes, onions and dates in a food processor until slightly chunky or smooth if you prefer.
2. Add remaining spices and pulse or mix in a bowl until blended.
3. Spread sauce onto bread squares on a baking sheet
4. Add toppings and warm in the dehydrator for 1 hour or until warm.
5. Serve immediately

Dessert

BANANA SPLIT

Yield: 1 serving

Equipment: Homogenizing juicer [I use a Green Star®], blender or food processor

Ingredients:

1 large fresh banana

1-2 frozen bananas

½ cup frozen strawberries

½ cup frozen peaches or other fruit

½ cup chocolate sauce

Instructions:

1. Slice the fresh banana in half length-wise
2. Make a basic ice cream by pushing each of the frozen fruits, separately, through a homogenizing plate in the juicer or by processing it in a blender or food processor. (A little water may need to be added to the blender or processor and then freeze it again for a stiffer mixture.)
3. Chop up some colorful fresh fruit for toppings.
4. Scoop out each flavor of ice cream you make and put them on the cut banana in a dish.
5. Sprinkle the fresh fruit toppings and drizzle with the chocolate sauce [recipe below].
6. Indulge yourself!

CHOCOLATE SAUCE

Yield: 1 cup

Equipment: saucepan

Ingredients:

½ cup raw honey

4 Tablespoons coconut oil, melted on low heat (watch so it doesn't get hotter than your finger)

½ cup cacao powder

Dash salt

2 teaspoons vanilla

* For a minty taste add 5-10 drops Purify® peppermint essential oil depending on how minty you like it (optional) – this goes in after it is off the heat if using the honey.

Instructions:

1. If using honey, warm in a saucepan on low with the coconut oil.
2. Take off heat and add remaining ingredients.
3. Drizzle over ice cream.

SATURDAY

MUESLI WITH ALMOND MILK

Yield: 8 servings
Equipment: Dehydrator
Ingredients:

4 cups raw rolled oats

2 cups mixed raw, unsalted pecans, pumpkin seeds and macadamia nuts or other nuts of your choice, soaked overnight and drained

1 cup coconut, shredded

1 teaspoon coconut oil

½ cup raw honey or organic maple syrup

1 cup each currants, raisins and dried cranberries

1 teaspoon cinnamon

Instructions:

1. Chop all nuts in processor until small chunks.
2. Mix all other ingredients together in a bowl with the nuts.
3. Spread on a Teflex® sheet and dehydrate 6-8 hours or overnight, until dry.
4. Place in an airtight container in the cupboard for 1-2 weeks or the refrigerator or freezer up to 3 months.
5. Eat as a cereal with Almond Milk [recipe on page 41] or use as a topping for desserts.

Snack

PROTEIN BARS

Yield: 12 servings
Equipment: Food processor
Ingredients:

2 cups raw walnuts
1 cup raw pecans
10 raw Brazil nuts
½ cup flax seeds, ground
¼ cup hemp seeds
¼ cup raw sesame seeds
¼ cup raw sunflower seeds
¼ cup raw pumpkin seeds

½ cup Medjool dates, pitted
½ cup dried apricots, diced
1/8 cup macadamia oil or coconut oil
1 ½ teaspoons cinnamon
¼ cup lemon juice
2 cups gluten-free rolled oats
½ cup coconut flakes, unsweetened
½ cup raisins, soaked

Instructions:

1. Soak all the nuts and seeds the night before. They can be soaked together in a large bowl of water.
2. In the morning, drain the nuts and seeds and chop in the food processor into small chunks. Put back into the bowl they were soaking in and set aside.
3. In the food processor, add the dates and apricots and process until small chunks. Add to bowl of nuts and seeds.
4. Mix in remaining ingredients and press down in a 9"x13" baking pan.
5. Refrigerate covered and cut into squares to serve.
6. These can be refrigerated or frozen for up to 3 months. Be sure to label and date.

Lunch

CUCUMBER ROLLS WITH GINGER SAUCE

Yield: 6-8 servings
Equipment: Mandolin, knife & cutting board
Ingredients:

Filling:

1 cup Boston lettuce or other green leafy lettuce, shredded

1 cup carrot sticks, julienned

½ cup Mung bean sprouts, rinsed

3 Tablespoons each basil, cilantro and mint leaves

1 teaspoon Thai hot pepper or other small chili pepper, seeded and julienned

'Rice' from Nori Roll [recipe on page 50]

Wrapper:

2 cucumbers, sliced very thin lengthwise using mandolin slicer (or you can hollow out chunks of cucumber as shown in the photo).

Sauce:

Thai Ginger Sauce [recipe on page 37]

Instructions:

1. Arrange your filling ingredients on a platter ready to use in the wraps.

2. Place a strip of cucumber on a board or table. Layer 2 Tablespoons each of lettuce and 2 Tablespoons of the 'rice' at one end of the cucumber. Then put 1 Tablespoon bean sprouts; 1 teaspoon each mint leaves, basil leaves and cilantro leaves; and 2 pieces of pepper along the remainder of the cucumber strip.

3. Place four julienned cucumber strips at both ends of the cucumber, roll the cucumber strips diagonally and place in a serving dish.

4. Repeat with remaining strips of cucumber and the rest of the filling ingredients.

5. Serve with the Thai Ginger Sauce. They are best served immediately but may be refrigerated up to 1 day after preparing.

TORTILLA CHIPS AND SALSA

Yield: 6-8 servings
Equipment: Dehydrator, food processor, coffee grinder

CHIPS

Ingredients:

1 ¾ cups flaxseed meal
4 cups frozen corn, thawed
¾ small red onion, diced
2 ½ Tablespoons olive oil
1 Tablespoon cumin
1 1/3 cups pure water

1 clove garlic, minced
¼ Tablespoon sea salt + extra for sprinkling
1 Tablespoon + 1 teaspoon fresh lime or lemon juice
Pinch cayenne
2 Tablespoons chili powder
1 Tablespoon hemp seeds

Instructions:

1. Grind flaxseeds in a coffee grinder for a meal. 1 ½ cups of seeds will make about 1 ¾ cups of meal.
2. In a food processor, chop the red onions and corn into small pieces and add remaining ingredients.
3. Spread batter onto a Teflex® sheet to about ¼" thickness.
4. Dehydrate about 45 minutes, remove from dehydrator and score them with a knife or spatula, being careful not to puncture the Teflex® sheet. *
5. Put back into the dehydrator overnight, about 12 hours.
6. Check the chips to be sure both sides are dry. If not, take another Teflex® sheet and put it over the top and turn the chips over. Remove the first sheet and allow to dry again in the dehydrator until crisp.

You can skip step 4 and just break them apart if you wish.

SALSA

Yield: 3 cups

Equipment: Knife and cutting board, food processor (optional)

Ingredients:

3-4 fresh tomatoes, diced

3-4 Tablespoons red or yellow onion, diced

1 clove garlic, minced

Handful cilantro, chopped fine

1-2 Habañero peppers, diced

1 small jalapeño pepper, diced (or more if you like it hotter)

1 Tablespoon sun-dried tomatoes, diced

Sea salt and pepper to taste

1 teaspoon cumin (optional)

Dash cayenne pepper (optional)

Instructions:

1. Combine all ingredients in a bowl and serve with chips and guacamole.

2. If it is too chunky, put into a food processor and pulse to get a smaller chunky salsa or for a longer time for a smoother salsa.

GUACAMOLE

Yield: 2 cups

Equipment: Food processor (optional)

Ingredients:

2 avocados, mashed

2 Tablespoons onion, diced fine

½ cup salsa [see recipe above]

1 Tablespoon lime or lemon, freshly squeezed

Sea salt to taste

Instructions:

1. Mash avocados and add remaining ingredients. For a smoother guacamole, process in the food processor until smooth.

Dinner

BROCCOLI AND RICE

Yield: 2 servings
Equipment: Food processor, high-speed blender (optional)
Ingredients:

Broccoli:

5 cups broccoli florets

2 Tablespoons lemon juice

3 Tablespoons olive oil

1 Tablespoon Bragg's Liquid Aminos or Coconut Aminos

1 teaspoon Kirkland's Organic No-Salt Seasoning

1 Tablespoon white onion, minced

Sauce:

¼ cup tahini [homemade recipe follows on page 78]

1 teaspoon lemon juice

1 teaspoon raw apple cider vinegar

3 teaspoons Bragg's Liquid Aminos or coconut aminos

½ clove garlic, minced

½ small chile, deseeded and diced

1 small cube ginger, minced

~ Ingredients and instructions continued on next page ~

Rice:

1 ½ cups parsnips, peeled and diced
1 ½ Tablespoons pine nuts
1 Tablespoon raw macadamia or cashew nuts
1 Tablespoon light miso paste
1 Tablespoon cold-pressed sesame oil
3 green onion sprigs, chopped fine
1 Tablespoon fresh parsley, minced fine

Instructions:
1. For broccoli, mix liquids together and marinade the broccoli florets as you massage them with your hands to break up the cell walls and allow the juices to get in. Let stand for 10 minutes while preparing the rest. The lemon juice actually chemically 'cooks' the broccoli.
2. For the sauce, combine all ingredients and blend in a high-speed blender or food processor until smooth. Put in a bowl. Set aside.
3. For 'rice,' grind all ingredients in a food processor until fluffy like rice. Transfer to a glass dish.
4. Combine the sauce and the broccoli and warm in the dehydrator in a glass dish for 1-2 hours.
5. Put the 'rice' in the dehydrator to warm for 1-2 hours.
6. To serve, put the warm rice on a plate and top with the broccoli and sauce. Enjoy!

HOMEMADE TAHINI
Yield: ½ cup
Ingredients:
¼ cup raw sesame seeds
1 teaspoon fresh lemon juice
1 Tablespoon olive or sesame oil
Dash sea salt
1 Tablespoon purified water

Instructions:
1. Put dry sesame seeds to your high power blender or food processor.
2. Add in sea salt and lemon juice.
3. Pulse until finely chopped and the oil starts to release. After a minute or two the consistency will become like nut butter.
4. Thin out the mixture by adding a high-quality unrefined sesame seed oil, olive oil or coconut oil in small quantities until the desired consistency is reached.

Dessert

COCONUT ICE CREAM

Ingredients:
Whipped Nut Cream [recipe on page 36]
1 Tablespoon lime juice, freshly squeezed

Instructions:

1. Blend ingredients together and freeze in a glass container with a lid.
2. When frozen, pass through a homogenizing plate in a juicer or you can put the mixture in an ice cream maker. Follow manufacturer's directions.
3. Scoop out and serve with fresh fruit, chocolate nibs, or Chocolate Sauce [recipe on page 71] or plain.

SUNDAY

Breakfast

MUESLI WITH APPLES AND COCONUT

Yield: 1 serving

Ingredients:

1 cup of recipe or leftovers of Muesli [recipe on page 72]

1 Granny Smith apple, diced or sliced thin into julienne strips

1/3 cup coconut, shredded and unsweetened

1/2 teaspoon cinnamon

1 cup almond or hemp milk

Raw honey to drizzle over the top

Instructions:

1. Mix all of the ingredients into a large cereal bowl.
2. Eat cold, or warm a bit in the dehydrator, about 30 minutes at 105 F.

Snack

OATMEAL COOKIES

Yield: About 2 dozen cookies
Equipment: Food processor
Ingredients:

2 cups raw rolled oats
1 cup coconut, shredded and unsweetened
¼ cup cacao nibs
½ cup dried cranberries or raisins (optional)
4 Medjool dates, pitted and diced small
1 teaspoon flaxseed meal
1 teaspoon cinnamon
1 cup coconut oil
¼ - ½ cup raw honey or maple syrup (depending on how sweet you want them)
2 teaspoons vanilla
1 pinch each sea salt and cayenne pepper

Instructions:

1. Soak the cacao nibs in water at least 10-20 minutes to soften.
2. Mix all dry ingredients in a medium bowl.
3. Mix all wet ingredients in a small bowl.
4. Add wet ingredients to dry ingredients and mix well. If smaller chunks are desired, pulse in a food processor a few times.
5. Form balls with a spoon or ice cream scoop and place on a parchment-lined baking sheet.
6. Freeze for 15 minutes or until firm.
7. These may be stored in the refrigerator or freezer up to 3 months.

Lunch

THAI COCONUT SOUP

Yield: 1-2 servings

Ingredients:

Soup Base:

Meat and water from one Young Thai Coconut
2 Tablespoons fresh lemon juice
1 tamarind, peeled and soaked in water
1 green onion, diced
½ clove garlic
1 teaspoon Curry Powder [recipe on page 37]
Cracked black pepper to taste
½ teaspoon chili powder
Pinch cayenne powder

Assembly:

½ cup red bell pepper, diced
½ cup celery, minced
2 Tablespoons green onions, minced

Instructions:

Blend all ingredients in a high speed blender until smooth and creamy. Taste to be sure it is seasoned well.

To assemble: Divide the soup among 4 bowls and garnish right before serving with the ingredients listed. Soup may also be poured back into the Thai coconut for presentation and eaten or served from there.

Snack

ALMOST RAW *GRAW*NOLA BARS

I was on Pinterest and I saw a recipe for "healthy" granola bars. They had lots of sugar and other ingredients. I would not consider healthy anything containing crispy rice. Did you know that most commercial crispy rice cereals have corn syrup in them? I use the puffed rice instead; not raw, but healthier.

Yield: 4-6 bars

Ingredients:

¼ cup raw honey

¼ cup coconut oil

2 cups rolled oats, cut up a bit in the food processor

3 Medjool dates, pitted and chopped

1 cup organic puffed rice cereal

½ teaspoon vanilla

½ teaspoon cinnamon

Optional: 2 Tablespoons raisins, chopped, or use cacao nibs. You can also add raw almond butter for a peanut buttery flavor.

Instructions:

1. Mix all ingredients in a bowl, then transfer to a lightly greased loaf pan and press down firmly.
2. Refrigerate until firm.
3. Cut into rectangles and serve.
4. They are so good, you may need to double the recipe and divide for different mix-ins to create a variety of flavors.

Dinner

MOCK MAC & CHEESE

Yield: 1 - 8"x 8" pan
Equipment: High-speed blender, spiralizer
Ingredients:

Cashew Cheese Sauce:

1 3/4 cups cashews, soaked 1-2 hours and drained

2 Tablespoons fresh squeezed lemon juice

1/8 cup almond milk

1 teaspoon sea salt

¼ cup nutritional yeast

¼ cup medium red onion

½ teaspoon chili powder

Pinch each turmeric and cayenne pepper

½ clove garlic

Crushed black pepper to taste

1 teaspoon Kirkland's® Organic No-Salt Seasoning

For Assembly:

4-5 yellow squash, peeled with ends cut off

Pinch sea salt

Finely chopped walnuts or pecans for topping

Chili powder & paprika (optional)

Instructions:

1. Blend all ingredients for cheese sauce in high-speed blender until smooth.
2. To assemble, make noodles out of the squash with a mandolin or spiralizer.
3. Roughly chop noodles into smaller strands and toss with a bit of salt. Let sit 30-45 minutes.
4. Mix noodles and cheese sauce in a bowl and spread into an 8"x 8" casserole pan.
5. Top with chopped nuts and extra chili powder or paprika.
6. Place in bottom of dehydrator at 115 F. for 1-2 hours to warm before serving.

Dessert

GREEN SMOOTHIE CREPES WITH WHIPPED NUT CREAM & FRUIT

Yield: 1-4 servings

Equipment: High-speed blender, dehydrator, nut milk bag or cheesecloth

Ingredients:

1 Green Smoothie Fruit Roll-up [recipe on page 39]

3 spoons full of Whipped Nut Cream [recipe on page 36]

1 ½ cups mixed fruit, strawberries, etc.

Instructions:

1. Place a roll-up on a plate and spread whipped cream down the center but not to the end on either side.
2. Sprinkle mixed fruit on top of the cream.
3. Fold both short ends at the top and bottom of the cream and roll the other longer sides to form a large cigar shape, like a burrito.
4. Spread more cream on top and sprinkle with remaining mixed fruit.

*If you want them more like fruit 'tacos' like in the photo, place the whipped cream on half of the roll-up and add the strawberries and peaches on top, then fold the other side over.

CHECK-IN FOR DAY 7:

Please complete this FIRST THING in the morning when you wake up!

On a scale of 1-10, with 10 being the best you can feel, how do you feel upon waking this morning? (Circle one) 1 2 3 4 5 6 7 8 9 10

Look in the mirror. How does your face look?

1. Blotchy and red
2. Puffy
3. Eyes swollen with dark rings around them
4. Other _____

Stick out your tongue. How pink is it?

1. It is not pink. It is white!
2. Quite pink with some white
3. A nice, clean pink with no white
4. Other _____

What kind of mood are you in?

1. Grumpy.
2. Tired. I want to go back to bed.
3. OK
4. Happy. I felt like I had a good night's sleep.
5. Energetic! I'm ready to take on the day!
6. Other _____

Please write down any other comments about things you notice upon waking this morning:

_____
_____
_____
_____
_____
_____
_____
_____
_____

COMPARE & SHARE

Compare the two Check-In sheets. What did you notice that was different **physically** from Day 1 to Day 7?

_____
_____
_____
_____

What did you notice that was different **emotionally** from Day 1 to Day 7?

_____
_____
_____
_____

What did you notice that was different **mentally** from Day 1 to Day 7?

_____
_____
_____
_____

What did you notice that was different about your **appearance** when you looked in the mirror from Day 1 to Day 7?

_____
_____
_____
_____

You just gathered **facts** to prove whether raw food actually works for you or not. Even the slightest differences can be noticed when you are paying attention.

Do you want more of this every day? Keep going with the menu plan each day and make more copies of the Check-in sheets to continue comparing the results, or turn to the next page to find out how you can get new recipes and experience with Raw Food.

CONGRATULATIONS!

You have successfully completed this

One Week Raw Food Challenge

Additional Recipes

CONTENTS

BREAKFAST

LUNCH

SNACKS

DINNER

DESSERT

Breakfast

NANA HEMP MILK

Yield: 2 ½ cups
Equipment: High-speed blender
Ingredients:
2 cups water
½ banana
½ cup hemp seeds

Instructions:
1. Blend ingredients in a high-speed blender.
2. Pour over your cereal or drink it up. Deliciously sweet and just the right consistency. Enjoy!

OMEGA 3 BREAKFAST PUDDING

Yield: 2 cups
Equipment: High-speed blender
Ingredients:
2 bananas
1 cup purified water
7 Medjool dates, pitted
½ cup walnuts, soaked 8 hours and rinsed
1 teaspoon cinnamon
1 Tablespoon flaxseed meal
1 teaspoon hemp seeds
½ teaspoon vanilla or scrape 1/8 section of a vanilla pod
1/3 cup coconut flakes, unsweetened (optional)

Instructions:
1. Blend all ingredients in a high-speed blender until smooth.
2. Will be warm from the machine after blending a couple of times. May eat warm, or cool in refrigerator first.
3. Fruit like blueberries or other berries would also be delicious as a topping to mix in. Enjoy!

OVERNIGHT OATMEAL

Yield: ¾ cup serving

Ingredients:

1/3 cup rolled oats

2 Tablespoons coconut flakes

3 Medjool dates, pitted and diced

1 green apple, diced with the skin on

2 teaspoons flaxseed meal

1 Tablespoon hemp seed

1/8 cup walnuts or pecans, soaked and diced

1 teaspoon cinnamon

Dash nutmeg

Instructions:

1. Place all ingredients in a thermos and mix well.
2. Add boiling water to the top.
3. Stir and cover with lid. Leave for 2 hours or overnight.

STRAWBERRY SMOOTHIE

Yield: 1 blender full

Equipment: High-speed blender

Ingredients:

3 Medjool dates, pitted

1 pint fresh strawberries with green tops on

4-5 large leaves fresh kale

2 bananas

Ice (optional)

Instructions:

1. Blend everything in a high-speed blender.
2. Add ice if you want it cold and enjoy!

BANANA ALMOND BUTTER BOWL

Yield: 2 cups
Equipment: Large bowl
Ingredients:
3-4 bananas
1 apple, diced (use green or red or whatever you have on hand)
Lemon juice
¼ cup almond butter, raw
Dash cinnamon

Instructions:
1. Layer all ingredients in order listed.
2. Top by sprinkling some fresh lemon juice and some cinnamon over the top.

CHIA JUICE

Yield: 1 cup
Ingredients:
1 cup organic fruit juice of your choice with no sugar added
¼ cup chia seeds

Instructions:
1. Mix chia seeds into the juice and refrigerate for at least one hour or until seeds have become the consistency of frog's eggs. Drink within a few days.

Lunch

AVOCADO SALAD

Yield: 1 serving
Ingredients:
1 bunch of spinach
½ avocado, diced
¼ red onion chopped
Small handful parsley, lightly chopped
1 lemon

Instructions:
1. Chop spinach into small pieces.
2. Place into a mixing bowl and mix with the remaining ingredients.
3. Serve in the bowl or on a dinner plate.

HOUSE SALAD

Yield: 6 servings
Ingredients:
1 to 2 garlic cloves
¼ teaspoon coarse sea salt
1 Tablespoon whole-grain mustard
2 Tablespoons honey
Freshly ground black pepper
2 Tablespoons balsamic vinegar
2 Tablespoons extra-virgin olive oil
6 cups mixed greens, such as arugula, Romaine lettuce, green leaf lettuce
½ cup pumpkin seeds, roasted and salted
Zest of 1 organic orange
2 oranges, peeled and sectioned
½ cup red onion, thinly sliced

Instructions:
1. In a large wooden bowl, mash the garlic cloves with the salt.
2. Add coarse ground mustard.
3. Whisk in the honey, pepper, vinegar and oil. Let stand 30 minutes.
4. Toss the greens, oranges, red onion and pumpkin seeds with the dressing.

INSALATA FLORENTINE

Yield: 4 servings

Ingredients:

½ cup julienne-shredded fresh spinach

2 Tablespoons ripe Roma tomatoes, diced

1 Tablespoon pine nuts, lightly toasted

1 Tablespoon sun-dried tomatoes, julienne cut

1 Tablespoon capers

1 Tablespoon black olives, sliced

1 Tablespoon radicchio, julienne-cut

¾ cup yellow squash, diced into very small pieces

3 ounces Roasted Garlic Lemon Vinaigrette [recipe below]

1 ½ teaspoons shaved Parmesan cheese or 1 teaspoon nutritional yeast if you want to remain vegan

Fresh cracked black pepper, for garnish

Instructions:

1. Place all ingredients except Parmesan cheese, in the order listed, in a chilled mixing bowl.
2. Lightly toss ingredients.
3. Garnish with shaved Parmesan cheese and fresh cracked pepper.

ROASTED GARLIC LEMON VINAIGRETTE

Yield: ½ cup

Equipment: Food processor

Ingredients:

¼ cup raw apple cider vinegar

3 Tablespoons raw honey

½ teaspoon sea salt

4-6 cloves garlic, roasted

¾ cup extra virgin olive oil

½ lemon, juiced

Instructions:

1. Place vinegar, honey, salt and roasted garlic in a food processor. Puree until the garlic is chopped very fine.
2. With the food processor still running, add olive oil and lemon juice.
3. Refrigerate until ready to use.

Be careful when 'roasting' the garlic. Do this on low heat with about 1 Tablespoon olive oil, just until the outside of the garlic cloves are slightly brown. You want to retain as much of the enzymes as possible but still get a good flavor from them.

LUNCH BOWL

Yield: 1 serving
Equipment: Food processor
Ingredients:
1 cup jicama, shredded
1 medium to large zucchini, diced with skin on
Juice of 1 lemon or 2 limes
4-5 cups fresh mixed greens
1 cup fresh tomato salsa [see recipe below]
½ avocado, diced
Small handful each, fresh cilantro and parsley

Instructions:
1. Shred jicama in a food processor to resemble rice.
2. Top the 'rice' with remaining ingredients in a large bowl. Enjoy!

PICO DE GALLO

Yield: 2 ½ cups
Ingredients:
2 cups fresh tomatoes, diced
½ cup red or white onion, diced
1 jalapeño, seeded and diced
Handful fresh cilantro, chopped
Juice from 2-3 limes

Instructions:
1. Combine all ingredients.
2. Serve with chips or use with other recipes.

MANGO PASTA

Yield: 4-6 servings

Equipment: Spiralizer®

Ingredients:

1-2 fresh yellow squash

2-3 ripe mangoes, peeled and seeded

Bunch of fresh parsley or mint

Instructions:

1. Using a Spiralizer®, make spaghetti-like noodles out of the fresh yellow squash by cutting off both ends, then cutting it in half. Place the squash half on the spiralizer and turn the handle away from you to make the noodles, allowing them to fall onto a plate.
2. Puree the fresh mangos in a blender until smooth.
3. Pour the mangos over the squash and mix until combined.
4. Transfer to a plate and sprinkle fresh parsley or mint over the top and enjoy the fresh flavors.

MEXICAN SOUP

Yield: 4 servings

Ingredients:

2 cups warm water

2 Roma tomatoes

½ large carrot

½ large celery piece

1" thick slice red pepper

¼ avocado (optional)

1 onion wedge

2 sprigs fresh cilantro

1 teaspoon Kirkland's® Organic No-Salt Seasoning

3/4 teaspoon garlic, minced

Instructions:

1. Add ingredients in the order listed into a high-speed blender.
2. Blend until smooth on the soup setting or until warm.

PEACH AND TOMATO SALAD
Yield: 4-6 servings
Ingredients:
4-6 large ripe tomatoes
4-6 large ripe peaches
Handful basil leaves, thinly sliced
Fresh lemon juice from 1 lemon (optional)

Instructions:
1. Slice tomatoes and peaches into slices or wedges and place on a large platter or in a bowl.
2. Sprinkle basil over the top and fresh lemon juice from 1 lemon. Enjoy!

PESTO STUFFED PIZZAS
Yield: 4-6 servings
Ingredients:
1 large zucchini
½ cup Basil Lemon Pesto [recipe follows]
Cherry tomatoes, sliced ¼ inch thick

Instructions:
1. Cut zucchini into ¼ inch rounds.
2. On each zucchini round, spread Pesto and top with tomatoes.
3. Enjoy these with a green salad.

BASIL LEMON PESTO
Yield: 1 cup
Equipment: Food processor or high-speed blender
Ingredients:
3 cloves garlic
¼ cup pine nuts
3 cups fresh basil leaves, slightly packed
Juice and zest of ½ a lemon

Instructions:
1. Place ingredients in a food processor or high-speed blender and blend until almost smooth. It is nice to have a little texture so pulse at the end to keep a few small chunks.
2. Serve with pasta.

SESAME MANDARIN ORANGE COLESLAW

Yield: 4-6 servings

Ingredients:

¼ head each purple and green cabbage, thinly sliced

2 mandarin oranges, peeled, chopped and seeded

¼ red onion, thinly sliced

4 Tablespoons fresh cilantro

2 Tablespoons fresh mint

2 Tablespoons raw sesame seeds

Instructions:

1. Put all ingredients in a large bowl or on a plate.
2. Dress with Thai Tomato Ginger Dressing [recipe follows].

THAI TOMATO GINGER DRESSING

Yield: 5 cups

Ingredients:

4-5 cups tomatoes

Small piece of ginger

1 cup celery, diced

½ cup sesame seeds

2 Tablespoons green onion, diced

½ clove garlic

Dash cayenne pepper (optional)

Ingredients:

1. Blend all ingredients until smooth.
2. Pour over Sesame Mandarin Orange Coleslaw [recipe above].

SUMMER SALAD

Yield: 2-4 servings

Ingredients:

1 package (10 oz) Spring Mix, washed
½ pint strawberries, sliced
3-4 oranges cut into wedges
1 cup celery, diced
1/8 cup red onion, diced (optional)
1/8 cup dried cranberries sweetened with natural juice (optional)
 you can get these in the bulk section at a health food store
¼ cup pecans, soaked 2 hours or overnight, drained and diced (optional)
½ to 1 recipe of the Summer Salad Dressing [recipe below]

Instructions:
1. Mix all ingredients together and pour a generous amount of the dressing over.
2. Toss together and enjoy as much as you can eat.

SUMMER SALAD DRESSING

Yield: 2 cups

Equipment: High-speed blender

Ingredients:

1 pint fresh strawberries with green tops on
2 bananas
3 Medjool dates, pitted
Juice of 1 orange

Instructions:
1. In a high-speed blender, blend all ingredients until smooth.
2. Pour over leafy greens or Summer Salad [recipe above] and enjoy.
   This recipe can also be made into a smoothie. Just add 1-2 cups of ice and blend until smooth. YUM!

THAI CUCUMBER SALAD

Yield: 4 servings

Ingredients:

¼ cup fresh basil, roughly chopped

2 medium cucumbers, julienned

1 head butter or bib lettuce, torn into small pieces

1 red bell pepper, julienned

1 yellow bell pepper, julienned

1 cup carrots, diced

1 cup celery, diced

½ cup green onions, diced

¼ cup mint leaves

Instructions:

1. Mix all salad ingredients together in a bowl.
2. Toss with Thai Ginger Sauce [recipe on page 37]. Thin recipe out with a little water if needed.
3. Serve in bowl or in individual portions on salad plates.

TRAIL MIX LUNCHBOX

Yield: 1 serving
Equipment: Large container
Ingredients:
½ pound Fresh figs
1 apple, red or green, whatever you have on hand

Trail Mix:
½ cup cashews
½ cup raisins
½ cup dried cranberries sweetened with juice (bulk section at Good Earth)
½ cup sunflower seeds
½ cup walnuts or pecans, soaked up to 8 hours in water, rinsed and dried
½ teaspoon cinnamon

Instructions:
Trail Mix:
1. Add all ingredients together and put in a separate container.
2. Seal, label and date.

Lunchbox:
1. Dice apples and figs.
2. Add in ¼ cup trail mix and sprinkle w/ cinnamon in large container

Snack

"ROASTED" PUMKIN SEEDS
Yield: 2-3 cups
Ingredients:
Pumpkin seeds from a fresh pumpkin

Seasoning of choice (I recommend Wild Tree® Italian Seasoning or an Italian seasoning blend of your choice.)

Instructions:
1. Cover wet seeds with seasoning of your choice.
2. Dehydrate in dehydrator at 105 degrees Fahrenheit.
3. Play around with different flavors using different seasonings that are sweet or savory.

LIME FRUIT

Yield: 1 pound
Ingredients:
1 pound mangoes or pears or honeydew melon, diced
Juice of 1 lime

Instructions:
Peel and slice desired fruit in a bowl and drizzle with lime juice.

PEACH SALSA

Yield: 1 ½ cups
Ingredients:
1 cup strawberries, diced
2 nectarines, diced
1 jalapeño pepper, seeded and finely chopped
1 Tablespoon red onion, finely chopped
2 Tablespoons fresh lime juice
1 Tablespoon fresh mint leaves, chopped
1 Tablespoon fresh cilantro, chopped

Instructions:
1. Mix all ingredients together.
2. Eat this by itself or on a bed of greens. You may also want to dip celery or other fresh vegetables in it like you would chips.

SLICED TOMATOES WITH FRESH BASIL & BALSAMIC

Yield: 4 servings
Ingredients:
2 to 3 ripe beefsteak tomatoes, sliced
½ cup fresh basil leaves
2 teaspoons balsamic vinegar (preferably aged)
2 teaspoons olive oil
Salt and ground black pepper

Instructions:
1. Arrange tomato slices on a plate and layer with basil leaves.
2. Drizzle vinegar and oil over them and sprinkle salt and crushed black pepper over top.

Dinner

RAW BURRITO

Yield: 2-3 servings
Equipment: High-speed blender
Ingredients:

Sauce:
Zucchini
2 colorful bell peppers
2-3 lemons or limes
Green onions
¼ cup sesame seeds
Cumin

Burrito:
Collard leaves, large
1 cup alfalfa sprouts
1 cup tomatoes
Handful cilantro
1 cup carrots, shredded
1 cup cucumber, shredded
¼ avocado for each burrito
Arugula leaves
Cherry tomatoes
Habaneros or jalapenos
3-4 olives

Instructions:

Sauce:
Blend zucchini, bell pepper, lemon, green onions, sesame seeds, cumin in a high-speed blender.

Burrito:
1. De-stem the collard leaf and thin off the thick part of the stem at the end. This is your 'tortilla.'
2. Spread the sauce onto the leaf, not quite to the edge.
3. Chop all remaining ingredients and add one by one onto the sauce.
4. Roll it like a burrito and put on a platter. Slice in half and enjoy!

CLASSIC GREEN SALAD

Yield: 6-8 servings

Ingredients:

¼ cup slivered almonds

2 Tablespoons organic sugar (optional)

1 pound green leaf lettuce

1 cup celery, chopped

¼ cup red onions, chopped

2-3 Mandarin oranges, peeled and sectioned

Pomegranate seeds (in season) from 1 pomegranate or 1 apple or 1 cup strawberries, diced

Dressing:

1/8 cup olive oil

1/8 cup water

2 Tablespoons raw apple cider vinegar

2 Tablespoons maple syrup

1 Tablespoon fresh parsley, chopped

½ teaspoon sea salt

Dash ground pepper

Dash cayenne pepper

Instructions:

1. Place almonds and sugar in a small saucepan and stir over medium heat until the sugar melts to coat the almonds. (This step may be omitted if you do not want the added sugar. Just add the almonds in at the end.) Cool on a parchment paper and set aside.
2. Tear lettuce into bite-sized pieces. Put in a large bowl and add celery, onion, and oranges. Add pomegranate seeds (in season) or other fruit of your choice like a diced apple or some strawberries.
3. Prepare dressing with ingredients listed in a blender or bottle and shake until combined. Toss salad with dressing, add almonds and toss just before serving.

CRANBERRY PUMPKIN SALAD

Yield: 4-6 servings

Ingredients:

1 head Treviso or radicchio, halved with the core intact
4-5 heads Belgian endive, halved with the core intact
¼ cup dried cranberries
¼ cup shelled pumpkin seeds, unsalted

Instructions:

1. Place all ingredients in a bowl or on a platter.
2. Top with Cranberry Orange Rosemary Dressing [see recipe below].

*If you are unable to find these kinds of lettuces, use whatever greens you have on hand.

CRANBERRY ORANGE ROSEMARY DRESSING

Yield: 5 cups

Ingredients:

3-4 cups oranges
½ cup fresh cranberries
1 cup Medjool dates, pitted
1 Tablespoon fresh rosemary

Instructions:

1. Blend all ingredients in a blender until smooth.
2. Pour the amount you want over salad.

BALSAMIC VINAIGRETTE DRESSING

Yield: 1 cup

Ingredients:

¼ cup balsamic vinegar
2 teaspoons maple syrup
½ teaspoon sea salt
1 Tablespoon garlic, minced
½ teaspoon fresh ground pepper
½ cup extra virgin olive oil
¼ cup water

Instructions:

Mix together in a bowl and serve over salad. This will keep in the refrigerator for several weeks.

FETTUCINI ALFREDO

Yield: 4-6 servings

Equipment: Spiralizer

Ingredients:

5 zucchini

¼ cup pine nuts

10 basil leaves

3-5 sage leaves

Oregano

1 clove garlic

½ head of cauliflower (optional)

Tomato, chopped and basil leaves for garnish

Instructions:

1. Blend pine nuts, basil, sage, oregano, and garlic together in high-speed blender.
2. Spiralize the zucchini noodles and put into a bowl.
3. Add the sauce onto the noodles. Mix in fully.
4. Take ½ a head of cauliflower and process until it becomes like 'snow.' It is the cheese you can put onto the top. Sprinkle on as if you would the cheese.
5. Garnish with tomatoes and basil leaves.

THREE INGREDIENT ZUCCHINI PASTA

Yield: 1 serving

Equipment: Spiralizer®

Ingredients:

1-2 zucchini or yellow squash

1 cup heirloom tomatoes, chopped

¼ cup parsley, chopped

Instructions:

1. Cut ends off zucchini or squash. Cut in half and put each half in a Spiralizer® to make noodles and put on a plate.
2. Top with chopped tomatoes and parsley and eat slowly, paying attention to the many flavors of this simple dish. Your taste buds will thank you and so will your digestive system!

PAD THAI

Yield: 4 servings

Equipment: Spiralizer®

Ingredients:

4-5 cups zucchini, shredded

1-2 cups carrots

1 cup red bell pepper

1 cup red cabbage

1 ½ cups mung bean sprouts

1 cup green onions, sliced

½ cup Portobello mushrooms, sliced (optional)

¼ cup fresh cilantro, chopped

¼ cup fresh parsley, chopped

¼ cup pistachio, crushed, for garnish

Thai Ginger Sauce [recipe on page 37]

Instructions:

1. Using a Spiralizer®, create long noodles with the jicama root. This may also be done with a knife or mandolin in julienne strips. Set aside.
2. Toss other ingredients together in a bowl & pour ½ the sauce over 'noodles' and toss until thoroughly mixed in.
3. To plate, spread a small amount of the sauce on a plate or serving dish. Top with a large amount of the noodles with sauce piled up into a mound, and drizzle noodles with remaining sauce.
4. Garnish with some pistachios and fresh parsley

POMEGRANATE SALAD

Yield: 2-4 servings

Ingredients:

Cinnamon-Sugared Almonds:

¼ cup almonds, slivered

1 Tablespoon maple syrup

¼ teaspoon cinnamon

Salad:

1 cup celery, chopped

3 green onions, sliced

1 can mandarin orange wedges

Pomegranate seeds

Dressing:

¼ cup grapeseed oil

2 Tablespoons vinegar

2 Tablespoons maple syrup or honey

1 Tablespoon fresh or dried parsley

½ teaspoon salt

Dash cayenne pepper

Dash ground black pepper

Instructions:

Cinnamon-Sugared Almonds:

1. Mix almonds, maple syrup and cinnamon together.
2. Dehydrate for 1 hour.

Salad:

1. Combine all salad ingredients in a medium-sized bowl.
2. Add almonds and lightly toss.

Dressing:

1. Mix together all dressing ingredients.
2. Serve with the pomegranate salad.

VEGETABLE PASTA WITH MARINARA SAUCE

Yield: 2 ½ cups

Equipment: Food processor, Spiralizer®

Ingredients:

Marinara Sauce:

2-3 large tomatoes, diced (garden fresh tomatoes are the best tasting)

1 clove garlic, minced

¼ small onion, diced

1 Medjool date, pitted

Fresh herbs: basil, oregano, thyme, parsley to taste (about 2-3 Tablespoons of each depending on your preference)

½ large red, yellow or orange bell pepper or about 2-3 small ones, diced

Real or sea salt and ground pepper to taste

Veggie Pasta:

Zucchini, yellow squash, or other favorite vegetables

Instructions:

Marinara Sauce:

1. Put date in food processor and process until mashed.
2. Add tomatoes and remaining ingredients and pulse until small chunks appear.
3. This may be warmed and put over vegetable noodles like zucchini or yellow squash. Use your finger as a thermometer. Anything that is too warm for your finger is too warm for the enzymes and will kill them.

*Be sure to taste the recipe before you serve to adjust the seasonings. ENJOY!

Veggie Pasta:

1. Using a spiralizer, cut zucchini or yellow squash or other vegetables into noodles.
2. Pour fresh marinara over the top and serve.

RAINBOW PASTA SALAD

Yield: 1 large serving
Equipment: Vegetable peeler and knife
Ingredients:
1 yellow squash
1 zucchini squash
1 carrot
1 cucumber
¼ cup Kalamata olives
1 cup cherry tomatoes, cut in half
¼ of a red onion, sliced

Instructions:
1. With a vegetable peeler, peel off strips from each of the vegetables.
2. Add the olives whole or cut in half, tomatoes and red onions.
3. Mix together and toss with favorite vinaigrette dressing.

Dessert

APPLE CINNAMON CREPES

Yield: 2-4 servings
Equipment: High-speed blender
Ingredients:

Crepes:

3 cups Thai coconut meat
1 ½ cups Granny Smith or other type of apples, chopped with peels on
½ -1 cup coconut water
1 ½ cup flaxseed meal
1 Tablespoon hemp seeds
3 Tablespoons organic maple syrup
2 teaspoons ground cinnamon
1 teaspoon sea salt

Apple Pecan Filling:

4 cups Granny Smith apples, diced with skins on (about 4 apples)
½ cup pecans, chopped coarsely
¼ cup currants (golden raisins), chopped or Medjool dates, diced or dried cranberries
3 Tablespoons organic maple syrup
3 Tablespoons fresh lemon juice

~ Ingredients and instructions continued on next page ~

½ teaspoon lemon zest, grated (zest the lemons first before juicing)
½ teaspoon ground cinnamon
¼ teaspoon sea salt
Dash nutmeg

Maple Whipped Cream:
½ cup coconut meat from a Thai coconut
¼ cup water from Thai coconut
½ cup maple syrup
2 Tablespoons coconut oil or butter
1 teaspoon vanilla

Instructions:
Crepes:
1. In a high-speed blender, add the coconut meat and apple and ¼ cup of the water at first, then add another ¼ cup at a time as the mixture is blending. You may need to stop the machine and use a spatula to scrape down the sides.
2. Transfer the coconut mixture to a large mixing bowl and add the remaining ingredients. Mix with a large spoon until completely combined.
3. Divide the batter between three to four 14" Teflex®-lined dehydrator trays. Spread the batter about 1/8" thick with an angled spatula toward the edges in a circular shape, about 4" in diameter.
4. Dehydrate at 105 F. for 6-8 hours or overnight. Flip over and peel the Teflex® off and place back onto the mesh liner to dehydrate for another hour or two until the underside is dry and the crepes are still pliable.

Apple Pecan Filling:
1. Place all ingredients in a bowl and toss until covered.
2. Spread on a Teflex®-lined dehydrator tray and dehydrate at 105 F. for about 2 hours until the apples soften and warm a bit.

Maple Whipped Cream:
1. In a high-speed blender, blend all ingredients thoroughly and transfer to a bowl.
2. Refrigerate for at least 1 hour and refrigerate remaining leftovers.

Assembly:
1. Fill each crepe with the apple filling and fold or roll up. Put on an individual plate or together on a platter for a crowd.
2. Serve with a dollop of maple whipped cream and drizzle some of the maple syrup over each crepe.

BANANA SPLIT POPS

Yield: About 12 pops

Ingredients:

3 cups coconut kefir

1 cup coconut palm sugar or ¾ cup maple syrup

3 medium ripe bananas, mashed, about 1 cup

¼ cup fresh lemon juice

2 teaspoons vanilla

1/8 teaspoon sea salt

1 cup fresh strawberries, chopped

¾ cup cacao nibs, soaked 15 minutes and drained

Instructions:

1. In a medium bowl, combine kefir, palm sugar, bananas, lemon juice, vanilla and salt until smooth.
2. Stir in strawberries and cacao nibs.
3. Divide mixture among 15-16 (3 oz.) paper drink cups. Cover each cup with a square of foil. Pierce the foil and insert a wooden craft stick into the mixture. Freeze for 4-24 hours.
4. Remove from freezer and let stand for 15 minutes. Tear away paper cups before serving.

This may also be made in popsicle molds.

CHERRY CHEESECAKE

Yield: 6-8 servings

Equipment: Food processor, juicer and blender or a high-speed blender, cheesecake or spring form pan, platter

Ingredients:

Crust:

2 cups mulberries

2 ½ cups dried figs

1 cup Medjool dates, pitted

½ teaspoon cinnamon

Cake:

2 cups cashew milk

7-10 ripe, frozen bananas

½ teaspoon cinnamon

1 teaspoon vanilla

Cherry Glaze:

3 pounds ripe cherries, pitted

1 ½ cups Medjool dates, pitted

Instructions:

Crust:

1. Add all ingredients into food processor and blend until crumbly.
2. Press into spring form pan with parchment on bottom.

Cake:

1. Make cashew milk according to directions below.
2. Add remaining ingredients in a high speed blender and blend until smooth.
3. The frozen bananas will give the mixture an ice cream-like consistency. Put in the freezer.

Cherry Glaze:

1. Blend up the cherries and dates in a food processor or high-speed blender until smooth.
2. Swirl half the cherry glaze into the frozen banana mixture just a little, then pour into crust. Pour the remaining cherry glaze on top and place back in the freezer.
3. Take out of the freezer when ready to serve and put fresh cherries all over the top. Cut into slices and enjoy.

Cashew milk: Soak 2 cups cashews in water for 20-30 minutes, then rinse. Blend in high-speed blender with 2 cups purified water. You can use the pulp from the milk as a crust in another dish, so do not discard. (This creates 2 cups cashew milk.)

LAVENDER ICE CREAM

Yield: 4-6 servings

Equipment: High-speed blender

Ingredients:

Water and meat from 1 large or 2 small Thai coconuts

½ vanilla pod, scraped

1 drop lavender essential oil (I prefer Purify® Essential Oils)*

1 cup fresh blueberries

8-10 Medjool dates

½ cup fresh blueberries for topping

¼- ½ teaspoon lavender buds

Instructions:

1. In a high-speed blender, blend all the ice cream ingredients until smooth.
2. Freeze in a glass dish with a lid. Allow to thaw slightly before serving in dishes.

See resource section for more information.

EGGNOG SHAKE

Yield: 2 cups
Equipment: High-speed blender
Ingredients:
½ cup almonds, soaked and rinsed
¼ cup Medjool dates, pitted
½ teaspoon pure vanilla
1 teaspoon cold-pressed coconut oil
1 teaspoon cinnamon
Dash nutmeg
1 cup purified water
Ice (optional)

Instructions:
1. Put everything in a high-speed blender and blend until smooth.
2. Drink immediately.

RAW HOT CHOCOLATE

Yield: 1 ½ cups
Ingredients:
½ cup Thai coconut meat
3 Medjool dates, pitted
3 teaspoons cacao powder
¼ teaspoon vanilla
1 cup Thai coconut water
Dash of cinnamon
Mint essential oil (optional)

Instructions:
1. Put everything into a blender and blend until smooth and it starts to warm the mixture.
2. Put into a mug and add a drop of mint essential oil if you like mint. Delicious!
3. Add whipped cream if desired or drink as is.

JUMBO FORTUNE COOKIES

Yield: 2 dozen cookies
Equipment: High-speed blender or food processor and dehydrator
Ingredients:
1 1/8 cups flax meal
1/8 cup hemp seed meal
¾ cup pear, chopped with skin on or apple, peeled
1/8 cup zucchini, shredded
½ cup young Thai coconut meat
2 teaspoons fresh lemon juice
1/3 cup maple syrup
½ teaspoon sea salt
1 teaspoon vanilla
¾ to 1 cup purified water

Instructions:
1. Blend all ingredients in a high-speed blender until smooth.
2. Add water until batter is pasty but still thick.
3. Spread into 3" circles on a Teflex® sheet and dehydrate 6-8 hours until firm but still pliable.
4. Place a fortune note on top of each cookie (look them up on google), with the end of the note barely hanging over the edge.
5. Carefully transfer to dehydrator trays and form into fortune cookie shapes, by folding in half, then folding again to pull down pointed edges. Use paper clips so secure edges if needed.
6. Dehydrate another 18-24 hours until crisp.

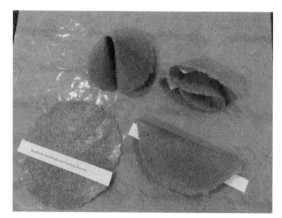

MY FAVORITE BROWNIES

This is my favorite recipe for Raw Brownies. I got it from a dear friend who I used to be in a Raw Food club together with. We would get together once a month and bring various Raw Food dishes to taste and share recipes. These brownies were the hit one month and continue to be the star of the show when I bring them to any party or teach them at my classes. They are rich, chocolaty and so easy to make!

Yield: 1 pan (about 24 small bites)
Equipment: Food processor
Ingredients:
2 cups Medjool dates, pitted
2 cups walnuts or pecans, soaked overnight and drained
½ cup cacao powder

Instructions:
1. In a food processor, blend up the dates until smooth and they form a paste. A ball will form and spin around the food processor bowl. Take out the dates and put into a bowl.
2. Chop up the walnuts in the food processor until ground fine.

~ Instructions continued on next page ~

3. Put the date paste back in the food processor with the nuts and add the cacao powder. Blend until smooth.
4. Put into a glass 8" X 8" brownie pan and press into the bottom and sides of the pan. You do not need to grease the pan.
5. Refrigerate and make the frosting [recipe below].

CHOCOLATE MINT FROSTING:

Yield: 1 cup
Equipment: Food processor
Ingredients:
½ – 2/3 cup raw honey or organic maple syrup
½ cup cacao powder
Dash salt
¼ teaspoon cinnamon
2 teaspoons vanilla (I use vanilla powder or vanilla without alcohol)
4 Tablespoons coconut oil
2-3 drops mint essential oil (optional)

Instructions:
1. Combine all ingredients in the order listed in food processor and blend until smooth, about 1 minute.
2. Spread on top of brownies and refrigerate until firm. Cut into small pieces and serve.

Raw Chef Wendy's Tip:
These brownies are rich, so I make them into small brownie bites and place them on a plate or tray to serve. They are great any time of the day for a snack or dessert.

RESOURCE GUIDE

I have been searching high and low the past 5+ years for help with various issues I have dealt with. I understand that our food, even the organic kind, is not grown in rich, nutrient dense soil and we have become deficient. We do the best we can with organic foods, but I found that I was still deficient in some areas. The following are resources for you if you feel you need them. They are companies and products that I have used and I love. I feel confident in recommending them because they have worked for me. If you have any questions about them or how to order them, please contact me at RawChefWendy@gmail.com

ESSENTIAL OILS ** There are many essential oils companies out there, but the quality varies greatly. The #1 word you need to see on the label is ORGANIC. If it doesn't say Certified Organic, then it isn't. The essential oils are the life blood of the plant and they are a very concentrated form - up to 100 times! The body utilizes the essential oils immediately and it uptakes all of the extras like pesticides, toxins and sewage sludge with it, if it is NOT Certified Organic or Wild Crafted (even better than organic because they are not farmed, but taken from the wild where the plants have not been sprayed and they are in their natural environment).

I recommend the essential oils from Purify Skin Therapy®. They are Certified Organic and Wild Crafted and are sourced by Holly Draper, the only Medical Aroma Therapist in the State of Utah. She is highly educated on the safety, use and efficacy of essential oils. After using essential oils from upwards of 6 different companies, these are the only ones I will use. You can order them at great prices from this link: http://www.purifyskintherapy.com/?Click=286

WARNING: Many companies teach that it is fine to put essential oils on infants and children of all ages. Holly teaches that Peppermint essential oil can suffocate an infant and cause them to stop breathing. DO NOT USE PEPPERMINT ON A CHILD UNDER 3 YEARS OF AGE! To adjust the mint recipe for a small child, please just use the mint leaves. You may use a few more to get the desired taste, but do not use the oil. Educate your family and friends about this danger and please come to Holly's classes to learn more or visit her website at the link above.

RECOMMENDED SUPPLEMENTATION

When I first began eating, I was a sugar addict and was attempting to get off of processed foods, so I naturally replaced the sugar with fruit. The problem was, I also had a yeast overgrowth, or Candida. This was very uncomfortable for me and difficult to control. If you don't know what this is or the symptoms associated with it, they can be as follows:

FOR MEN: Athlete's foot, fungus in fingernails and toenails, jock itch, etc.;
FOR WOMEN: Fungus in fingernails and toenails, vaginal itching and discharge anywhere from a thin yellow color to a thick cottage cheese appearance.

These and other symptoms can occur when the body is out of pH balance. This has to do with the amount of acid or alkalinity we have in our system. We need a more alkaline than acid environment: 7.2 on the pH scale is about neutral. The more acidic we are, the more prone to sickness and disease we become. Colds and flu are a bit more acidic and cancer is very acidic.

This has a great deal to do with what we eat and it can be difficult to achieve a consistent balance with food alone. That is why I highly recommend the Purium® products. They are great for supplementation for nutrition that we are lacking and to help keep the pH balanced. Because of the pesticides, hormones, lack of nutrients in the soil and toxins in the air and water, we need some help to maintain balance.

After being approached by multiple companies and trying hundreds of products from the store shelves and other companies, I have chosen a company with the highest quality products I can find. They are certified organic, non-GMO, raw, soy-free, gluten-free, and are delicious. I consider these concentrated nutrients that can replace some meals. The greens are sprouted and have a very impressive amount of nutrients. I put these together with a banana in my shakes in the morning.

To learn more about the products and the company, visit:

mypurium.com/rawchefwendy

$50 Gift Card

If this is the first time you have been introduced to Purium®, please use the gift card code: *rawchefwendy* to receive your first $50 off otherwise, use the gift card code given to you by your friend who introduced it to you.

For a list of books I recommend, please visit:

http://astore.amazon.com/rawchefwendyc-20

For a list of equipment I recommend, please visit:

http://astore.amazon.com/equipmentandtools-20

The next step is to attend a series of classes with…

… to learn how to prepare even more delicious Raw Food!
It's time to invest in your health for prevention and to enjoy a
richer lifestyle full of energy and fun!

Please check www.RawChefWendy.com/events for class dates and times.

THERE IS MORE AVAILABLE TO SUPPORT YOU

More Books
Online Programs
Private Chef Courses
Little Chef Summer Camp
Online Market
Monthly Newsletters
Magazine Articles
Television Appearances
Conferences
Retreats
& Much More!

Visit www.rawchefwendy.com and get involved.